# Strategic Governance

# Strategic Governance

*Enabling Financial, Environmental, and Social Sustainability*

By
**Hank Boerner**
and
**Mark W. Sickles**

*Fellows*
*Governance & Accountability*
*Institute*

PUBLISHER

215 Park Avenue South, 10th Floor
New York, New York 10003

Tel / Fax 646.430.4230 | Email info@ga-institute.com

Web www.ga-institute.com

# Strategic Governance
Enabling Financial, Environmental, and Social Sustainability

First Edition – October 2010

Copyright © 2010 by Mark W. Sickles

All Rights Reserved, including the right of reproduction in whole or in part in any form by electronic or mechanical or other means without permission of the authors and publisher. Exceptions for reviewers who wish to quote brief passages in connection with a review prepared for a publicly-available medium.

For information about permission to reproduce selections from this book please email: info@ga-institute.com

Library of Congress ISBN 978-0-615-40829-3
Library of Congress Copyright Office Registration, 1-472624641
United States Patent and Trademark Office, Serial Number 85137295

Boerner, Hank and Sickles, Mark W.

1 - Strategic Governance (title), 2- Corporate Governance, 3 - Corporate Strategies, 4 - Corporate Culture

Published by Governance & Accountability Institute, Inc.
Offices at 215 Park Avenue South, New York, NY 10003
Tel: 646-454-8230 email: info@ga-institute.com

Trademark Information: "Strategic Governance" is the methodology representing the body of work of Mark W. Sickles developed over three-decades in business. Mark W. Sickles is the creator of the "Strategic Governance" approach (book, service, and software), which has been produced in collaboration with the Governance & Accountability Institute.

The boxed impression of the globe with check mark and outline of symbols in chalked format is the trademark of Governance & Accountability Institute, Inc. Registration applied for.

# TABLE OF CONTENTS

Preface ................................................................. ix

Introduction ........................................................... xv

Making the Case:
The Need for a Global Governance Standard ..................... 1

The Universal Purpose of Corporate Governance ................ 9

How to Respond to Challenges – Internal and External ...... 15

Summary ............................................................... 75

The Top Ten Principles of
Strategic Governance ............................................... 77

Conclusion ............................................................ 85

Strategic Governance Related Quotes .......................... 87

Appendix .............................................................. 99

Acknowledgments ................................................. 107

About Governance & Accountability Institute ................ 111

About the Authors ................................................. 112

# PREFACE
# The Strategic Governance System

This book, *Strategic Governance*, is part of a whole. Specifically, the complete Strategic Governance System (SGS) is a three-legged stool consisting of "book, service, and software." As with all systems, the performance of this whole is greater than the sum performance of its parts. Furthermore, SGS is a permutation in which sequence counts. The intended order of progression is book, followed by service, followed by software. To read this book is to begin a journey leading to financial, environmental, and social sustainability.

Strategic Governance System: A Three-Legged Stool

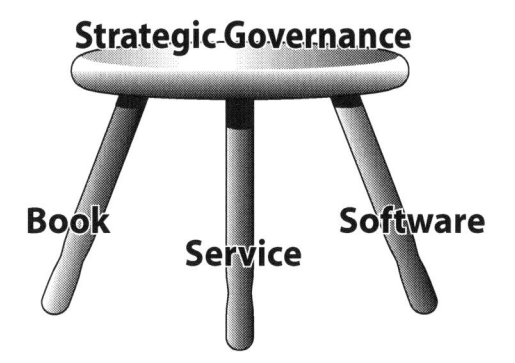

Copyright 2010, Mark. W. Sickles

## The Book

*"We cannot solve our problems with the same thinking we used when we created them."*

**Albert Einstein**

*"Man's mind stretched to a new idea never goes back to its original dimensions."*

**Oliver Wendell Holmes, Jr.**

This book is a unique opportunity to reorient your thinking about what's possible for your business by introducing you to an enlightened, principle-based governance regime. When you transform this new way of thinking into effective actions, you will achieve extraordinary results simply because this "new idea" driving your actions departs from conventional wisdom. For this reason, this book is also an opportunity to achieve sustainable competitive advantage.

## Service and Software

By allowing you to *think* yourself into a better way of *acting*, the book enables you to complete the first stage of your strategic governance and sustainability journey. The service leg of the SGS stool picks up where the book leg left off, leading you through the second stage.

**Strategic Governance Service**

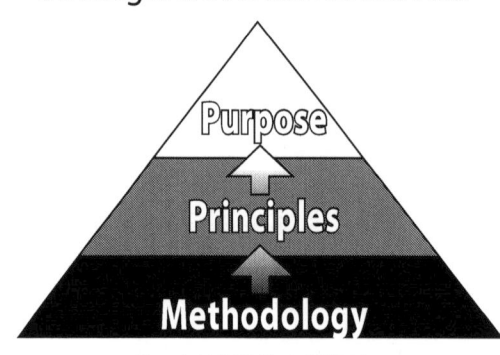

Purpose
Principles
Methodology

Copyright 2010, Mark. W. Sickles

In this next stage, you are guided through a principle-based process enabling you to *act* yourself into an even more advanced way of *thinking*. Then, in the third and final stage, the Strategic Governance Software will enable you to codify your new ways of thinking and acting into your organization's operating culture and daily work. This will ingrain Strategic Governance into your business environment, thereby assuring the "stickiness" essential to sustainability.

The overall SGS process is similar to the "4 Is" progression of the quality movement: Information (book), followed by Inspiration (effect of the book), followed by Implementation (service), and finally, Institutionalization (software). A brief summary of the Strategic Governance Service and Software is provided for your consideration on pages 102 and 104 in the Appendix.

## Strategic Governance Software (SaaS)

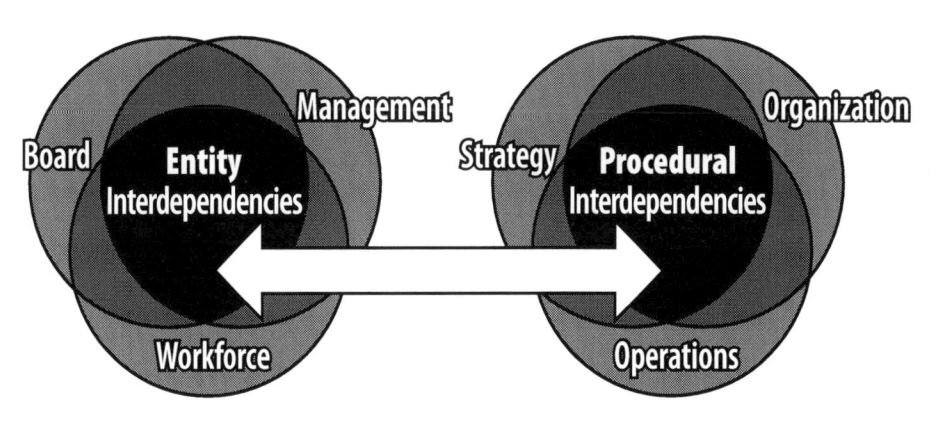

Copyright 2010, Mark. W. Sickles

## About Strategic Governance

> **Strategic Governance is a reorientation of the individual and global business community experience to account for the existence of an enlightened governance regime, the possibility of achieving it, and the availability of a principle-based system for doing so.**
>
> **Until this reorientation is complete, we can only wonder who the next Enron, Lehman or Goldman Sachs will be, and how our lives will be adversely affected.**

## About the Length of This Book

*Strategic Governance* is a short book that will not take long to read. We know that for you, the intended audience of business leaders and management professionals, time is a precious commodity. This reminds us of another short book, *Leadership is an Art*, authored by Max Depree, former CEO of furniture manufacturer Herman Miller based in Zeeland, Michigan. Mr. Depree said that, while his book will not take long to read, simply reading it is not the goal. The goal is to take *ownership* of the book's content, using the book as an ongoing source of continuous improvement.

Our message is the same: The purpose of *Strategic Governance* is not to dabble in it, but instead, master it by taking a radical and realistic look at what ails us, and what can now be done about it. That *will* take time and effort, and we promise an extraordinary return on this investment.

## About Our Approach

This book is a collaborative effort between two friends and Fellows of the Governance and Accountability Institute: Hank Boerner and Mark W. Sickles. Mark's areas of expertise include governance, strategy, sustainability, organizational effectiveness, and long-term shareholder value. He has worked in most industry sectors as an executive, officer, board member, consultant, and keynote speaker. Hank has deep experience in corporate governance, having been involved in more than 300 critical event or crisis episodes involving private, public and social sector organizations. Mark's and Hank's Bios appear in the section, About the Authors, on page 111.

The events shared in this book fall into three categories: Events experienced by Hank and Mark together; events experienced by Hank alone; events experienced by Mark alone. For "ease of reading" purposes, and also because all these events have been thoroughly discussed between the co-authors, these events will all be shared with you by "us" and "we," rather than "him" or "I."

## About Our Discipline

Strategic Governance as a body of knowledge has been developed over the years toward the goal of becoming a science. A body of knowledge becomes a science when, to paraphrase Albert Einstein, the need for proof of assertion decreases because of increases in its lucidity and logic. This is achieved by focusing on the triad of *what, why, and how.*

Several years ago, we gave a presentation on an earlier generation of Strategic Governance to an audience of senior executives.

Before doing so, we studied the evaluation form to learn how we were going to be judged by the audience. The first question, set up as a continuum, asked whether the presentation was "Practical" or "Theoretical." The way the scoring was set up clearly indicated that Practical was good and Theoretical meant "Impractical" and was bad. We addressed this with the audience by saying our presentation was both practical *and* theoretical, citing Dr. W. Edwards Deming's well-known thought that practice without theory is meaningless, adding that management is a paradox: A game of "and/both," not "either/or."

When a body of knowledge is practical (the *what*), supported by theory (*why*), and guided by principles (*how*), over time, axioms (*self-evident truths*) emerge. This is the goal of science, and management is a science. (To those who say management is an art, we agree, defining art as "the creative application of science" – and/both, not either/or.)

Over the last 30 years, we have followed this disciplined path on our ongoing journey of continuous improvement, leading to the development and evolution of the science of Strategic Governance into what it is today. By joining us on this journey, you will become a valued contributor to the growing momentum of the Strategic Governance movement enhancing the global business community's ability to achieve The Universal Purpose of Corporate Governance and thereby fulfill its destiny. If not you, who? If not now, when? Welcome aboard!

# INTRODUCTION

*"Imagination is more important than knowledge."*
**Albert Einstein**

Imagine a future in which your company is included in a mutual fund or Exchange-Traded Fund comprised of only the best-managed firms from each industry sector. Imagine in this future your company consistently outperforming all alternative investments of comparable risk. Imagine being considered a great company to partner with by your suppliers and vendors, a great company to work for by your employees, a great company to buy from by your customers, and a great company to invest in by your owners. Imagine a future where all of your valued stakeholders praise your ability to integrate and manage financial, social, and environmental responsibilities in ways that meet or exceed their needs and expectations. If you find this future desirable, then read on.

*Strategic Governance* is a unique approach for "pulling this future into the present" while developing your organization's overall capability into a strategic asset and sustainable competitive advantage. As a first step, we recommend taking the Strategic Governance Self-Assessment Survey now, before reading the rest of the book. (This survey appears in the Appendix on page 99 and online at http://www.SustainabilityHQ.com/SGSurvey.) Then, after reading the book and imagining your company transformed by the Strategic Governance System, we recommend taking the survey again from this new point of view, and then developing and implementing plans to achieve this transformation. Key point: The bigger the difference in the survey results, the bigger your opportunity for improvement.

# Making the Case: The Need For A Global Governance Standard

In October of 2008, activist investor Carl Icahn issued the public charge that corporate boards of directors aren't doing their jobs. Famed investor Warren Buffett in effect said the same thing in 2003. And as far back as 1976, no less an authority as modern corporate management's leading guru, the late Peter Drucker, observed that the corporate board of directors has failed as an institution in nearly every major financial fiasco over the last half-century or more. (Taking us all the way back to 1926!)

Having been deeply involved in board education and corporate governance during the first decade of this new century, we can see why: There has been far too little discipline and science applied to this critical function. Corporate governance, ironically, needs to be better governed, and the roles of directors, officers and managers need to be transformed.

The global economic crisis that took hold in early 2008 stands as an indictment of past and present governance approaches. Issuer box-checking, more financial legislation, and copious new federal regulations may indeed be necessary, but they are definitely not going to be sufficient over the long-term. **Something's missing, and it's been missing for a long time.**

Consider this conclusion reached by a task force of US-based political officials during the Clinton Administration: You can have a bad society with a good economy, but you can't have a good society with a bad economy, because you need the resources derived from that good economy to fund what constitutes a good society.

This conclusion begs the following question: What's been missing that needs to be present for communities and businesses to work together as a more harmonious system, to simultaneously and continuously create and maintain good economies *and* good societies?

**The answer, in a word, is *integrity*.**

By integrity, we mean a lot more than being honest. We mean soundness and wholeness of the business enterprise, achieved by leadership competence at the systems level of thought and action, often described as "leadership by design," or "leadership by architecture." **This leadership style has been missing, and it's been *missing* that it's missing!**

When integrity and the systems level of thought and action are present, you will manage your business as part of a community. You will include "assuring a good society" – providing the greatest amount of good for the greatest amount of people – as part of your firm's purpose.

And when your whole community prospers as a good society, there will be more qualified employees and suppliers, more able-to-buy customers, and more able-to-invest shareholders. Counter-intuitively, your giving to society will bring you and your stakeholders greater economic wealth.

As you know by now, there is a new community demanding our integrity – the global economy. If we fail to respond to the internal and external challenges we face, the economic fiascos of the first decade of this new millennium will continue, simply because the root cause of the problem is what's always been our most costly error of omission: **Failing to think and act at the systems level.**

Yes, as author Thomas Friedman writes, the world is now flat, in large part due to the dispersion of the wireless Internet. But no, the world is not yet a global eco-system, where all the parts work together in a state of integrity, harmoniously pursuing shared goals and objectives. All we have to do is look at the 2010 Goldman Sachs case to know we still have a serious problem to solve requiring a new, principle-based approach to corporate governance.

Again, something's missing that needs to be present. To repeat the key thought here: **That something is management at the systems level of thought and action.**

Historically, management as a discipline has not developed as rapidly as technology. This disparity has created a costly dysfunction summed up with this statement: *We think we're in the saddle riding technology, but instead, technology is in the saddle riding us.*

For example, while working with a *Fortune 200* durable goods firm several years ago, we heard that the senior members of the IT staff said to the CFO, "Good news – the SAP implementation is done." The CFO responded by asking, "If the SAP implementation is done, why aren't we doing our work any differently?" *We think we're in the saddle riding technology, but instead, technology is in the saddle riding us.*

Here's what everyone seems to be missing: It's more important to install the system in your people's *minds* than it is to install the system in your people's *computers*. The people at this durable goods firm were not doing their work any differently because, in their minds, their work had not changed. The new SAP software was not a solution to their problems, but instead, represented a distraction from their work. The technology was being *pushed* on line management by IT when it should have been *pulled* from IT by line management. SAP sold the technology to IT – but IT never bothered to sell the technology to line management.

We've seen this before. The CIO complains to the CEO that no one is using the new software system that cost the shareholders millions of dollars. So the CEO asks line management, "Why not?" The answer: "Because that's not the way we do our work!"

Our colleague, Barrie Peterson of Fairleigh Dickinson University, views this as leaders thinking that technology is some overarching, inevitable force rather than something people use too often for their own short-term or exploitative ends. The e-commerce bubble, he points out, was based on a fantasy that "eyeballs visiting websites" could be counted as future potential income and that fiber-optic, when laid down, could be booked by Enron as current profit.

In another *Fortune 500* firm – a leader in the food sector – we were asked to help members of a corporate function who felt they were being bullied by IT to change from PeopleSoft to SAP software. We asked them, "Do you feel your IT function is more interested in satisfying you or SAP?" They said, "That's the easiest question we've been asked in a long time." *We think we're in the saddle riding technology, but instead, technology is in the saddle riding us.* To reverse this trend, it is imperative to remember that, while *management without technology is lame, technology without management is blind.*

In 2009, on network television in the US, a teenage girl was asked why she put embarrassing pictures of herself on her personal website. She explained, "It's easy." The interviewer went back at her to clarify: "No, I'm not asking *how* you uploaded the pictures to your site; I'm asking *why* you did it, since they reflect so poorly on your character." The young woman could not hear the difference in the question, responding, "I already told you – it's easy."

When we shared this story with a university professor, a colleague who had been complaining that his students think editing a paper simply means using spell-check – *blindly* – we asked him if he had an explanation. He responded in a heartbeat: "They think if the technology lets you do it, it must be good."

In brief, as each of these tales indicates, we have insufficient management and excess technology. This imbalance causes blind usage of *technology* systems, arguably a significant factor contributing to the 2008 global economic crisis, due to the corresponding insufficient usage of *management* systems. The Strategic Governance movement will correct this imbalance.

For the most part, technology is an enabler, an accelerator, and potential source of error-free work. It enables us to do things we otherwise couldn't do, or do things we can do faster and more accurately. If we have a *bad* management approach, technology will accelerate our demise. If we have a *good* management approach – one based on integrity and the systems level of thought and action – technology will accelerate our success. So our focus should be on better management, which in this context also includes leadership and governance, to which our use of technology should apply.

Having considered the implications of our blind use of technology in our flat world, we can now gain new insights into the root cause of the global economic crisis.

## The Dysfunctional Heap

Our global economy is not yet an integrated *whole*; it's more like a dysfunctional *heap*. The parts are not aligned, linked, and working interdependently in pursuit of a "significant few" shared goals and objectives. Instead, these parts act as if they are independent wholes, with little or no concern about the effect their decisions and actions may have on others. There is too much emphasis on "local" optimization, and not enough emphasis on "enterprise" and "global" optimization.

But technology had connected these "independent" parts all around the world, so that a Sovereign Wealth Fund (SWF) in a nation-state far outside the traditional Wall Street business community was able to buy a package of mortgaged-back securities and "insurance policies" called derivatives. And we all know how that worked out! *If the technology lets you do it, it must be good.*

Since integrity was missing from management, the insurance policies were sold without the capital reserves needed to support them. The people who designed these instruments did not consider or care about the global implications of their imprudence.

The people who sold them to SWFs, foreign and domestic pension systems, and the world's central bankers, also did not consider or care about the consequences of the widespread potential default of these exotic products. Why?

Because what's been missing from management, from leadership, and from governance, is the essential ingredient for integrity, wholeness and soundness: **A principle-based, systematic, strategic approach to governance.**

This is why the Strategic Governance System we've developed includes 10 interdependent principles, themselves forming an integrated *whole.* When these principles are masterfully applied using a methodology proven to increase long-term shareholder value, The Universal Purpose of Corporate Governance is achieved, and the goal of a global eco-system becomes an opportunity to pursue, rather than a pipe-dream to dismiss. This is Strategic Governance in a nut shell: Methodology enabling principles; principles enabling purpose.

# The Universal Purpose of Corporate Governance

In the spring of 2009, we had the opportunity to serve as Chairman of the 3rd Annual MENA Region Corporate Governance Congress held in Dubai and sponsored by IIR Middle East. Due to the state of the global economy at that time, the *quantity* of attendees was down from the previous year, but the *quality* of those who did attend was exceptional. We responded to this opportunity by transforming the congress into a highly interactive discussion among this globally-diverse group of governance opinion leaders, influentials, and practitioners, producing what we all feel is a root-cause solution to past, present, and future economic crises: **The Universal Purpose of Corporate Governance.**

We began the congress by leading the group through an inquiry into the meaning of the following statement: *"A crisis is a terrible thing to waste."*

The group felt this statement meant we should look for opportunity in the face of adversity. As the saying goes, breakthroughs are often preceded by breakdowns, and we certainly, in 2008 and 2009, had the latter in our global capital markets, corporate sectors, and both global and local economies.

We then proposed that this is no time for the "tranquilizing drug of gradualism," no time for projecting the past forward, and no time for "business as usual." Instead, we asserted that this is a time for bold, decisive action, for declaring a future beyond business as usual, and for creating performance that cannot be predicted by anything done in the past. We suggested that declaring the future of corporate governance, and then "pulling that future into the present" with effective action, was not only an *opportunity* for those of us at the congress, but was our *responsibility* to the global business community. And so we did.

The congress culminated with our facilitating a process in which a combination of speakers and delegates representing every major region of the world produced **The Universal Purpose of Corporate Governance** (which we started developing in 2008 with Japanese governance expert and retired Hitachi board director, Go Sato).

This statement is based on the following six assertions:
- The four critical pillars of strategic governance are government, education, professional associations, and industry. (The familiar .govs, .edus, .orgs, and .coms)
- Government needs to coordinate with education and professional associations to provide guidance and support to industry.
- Industry values and standards need to be managed in the context of professional and ethical values and standards toward the goal of sustainability.

- The focus should be on the creation and management of firm-level cultures based on ethical, professional, and industry values and standards.
- The goal for industry and professional values and standards is to set the bar higher than ethical values and standards and governmental regulations, whose purpose is to serve as a safety net to prevent economic fiascos like *Enronitis* beginning in 2001, and the capital market crisis beginning in 2008.
- If a firm, unit, function, or individual is not conforming with all three categories of values and standards (ethical, professional, and industry), it is unethical to continue on that path. Governments should prevent this through regulation, legislation and enforcement.

These six assertions serve as the foundation for the following statement:

> **"The Universal Purpose of Corporate Governance is to integrate ethical, professional, and industry values and standards into firm-level cultures that enable winning strategies, manage risk, meet the needs and expectations of the firm's stakeholders, and fulfill the firm's responsibility for a sustainable world."**

One of the participants in this discussion was Professor Mervyn E. King, Chairman of the Board of Global Reporting Initiative (GRI). GRI is a network-based organization developing and managing the world's most widely-used sustainability reporting framework. This framework provides the global business community with principles and indicators for measuring and reporting on their financial, environmental, and social performance. (Note: The person with direct responsibility for developing and continuously improving GRI's sustainability framework is Mike Wallace, a co-fellow with us at the Governance & Accountability Institute.)

### Culture: The "Heart & Soul" of Corporate Governance

**Values and Standards**: Ethical | Professional | Industry

**CULTURE**

Winning Strategies | Managed Risk | Delighted Stakeholders | Sustainable World

Copyright 2010, Mark. W. Sickles

At the governance congress in Dubai, where Professor King served as the keynote speaker, he actively participated in a thorough review of the Top Ten Principles of Strategic Governance, and then, subsequent to the completion of the congress, helped finalize the definition of The Universal Definition of Corporate Governance as stated above.

The following year, in April of 2010, Professor King participated with us in a conversation recorded at the American Movie Company in New York City, where we discussed the synergistic relationship between GRI's sustainability framework and the Strategic Governance "three-legged stool" of book, service, and software. Specifically, both GRI and Strategic Governance focus on the integration of governance with strategy, risk, culture, and social responsibility. GRI's focus is on measuring and reporting or – in quality terms – "saying what you do", aka *talking the talk* of sustainability. On the other side of the sustainability coin,

Strategic Governance provides the global business community with an action-based system of methods, principles, and purpose to – again in quality terms – "do what you say", aka *walk the talk* of sustainability.

By integrating and leveraging the full value of Strategic Governance and GRI, firms are now able to "say what they do about sustainability, do what they say, and document it with openness, honesty, and integrity." The overall effect is a newly enlightened governance regime as described in the beginning of this book, made possible by the availability of a principle-based system for achieving it. All that's needed now is your effective action.

In our recorded conversation, available for viewing at www.ga-institute.com, you'll note that Professor King refers to organizations as "incapacitated people" requiring business leaders to act as their "hearts, minds, and souls." This view is consistent with our long-standing position that managing a business is like managing the human body, and that the primary role of leadership – those who work inside the boardroom – is to work *on* the business, installing the organizational equivalent of the human central nervous system needed to create so-called "smart organizations", in which *ordinary* people achieve *extraordinary* results.

Think of the boardroom and the people working in it as the brain of the business. This brain is connected to senior management, which serves as the spinal cord of the business. This spinal cord is then connected to all the nerve endings, which extend throughout the organization's body, representing the rest of management, down to the supervisory level. These nerve endings are ultimately connected to every cell in the body, which represent the overall workforce. Once installed by leadership, information and work can flow through this system of intelligence to achieve extraordinary results and thereby reflect favorably on the "hearts, minds and souls" of these leaders. This is the purpose of Strategic Governance.

# How To Respond To Challenges – Internal and External

*May we live in interesting times.*
– said to be an ancient Chinese blessing and curse.

As previously stated, this is not the time for incremental change. If your order of change is not big enough, the *status quo* will beat you down, causing you to fail your organization and its stakeholders as their leader. Instead, this is the time for strong leadership: bold, decisive action to fully utilize the Strategic Governance System's unique potential for creating extraordinary results for you, your firm, and its valued stakeholders. This can be done in a two-step process:

- Develop a deep understanding of the meaning and implications of The Universal Purpose of Corporate Governance
- Develop and implement your own unique purpose for corporate governance that aligns with The Universal Purpose, while providing your firm with a sustainable competitive advantage.

The primary system for taking these two steps is the Top Ten Principles of Strategic Governance:

1. The Essence of Governance
2. The Essence of Strategy
3. The Essence of Risk
4. The Relationship between Governance, Strategy, and Risk
5. The Relationship between Boards, Governance, and Shareholders
6. The Relationship between Boards, Management, and Shareholders
7. The Relationship between Boards, Strategy, and Culture
8. The Relationship between Boards, Management, and Strategy
9. The Essence of Culture
10. The Relationship between Organizational Design and Strategy

(These principles are described in detail beginning on page 77.)

The mastery and subsequent application of this proven system of interdependent principles – supported by a related system of models, methods, and techniques – will provide your enterprise with the holistic capability to fulfill The Universal Purpose of Corporate Governance.

This "systems level" of performance will enable and empower your firm to set and achieve internal standards far greater than any external criteria, and will complement the effective role of regulation, legislation, and enforcement: Assuring a principle-based approach to corporate governance. **This systems level of performance is what's been missing.**

As we all know, windows of opportunity don't stay open forever. Firms who can act quickly and effectively to take advantage of this new strategic lever will be the big winners, enjoying a sustainable competitive advantage over peers and competitors. Those who move with the herd may, over time, achieve competitive parity. And those who resist this change the longest will make the same effort and incur the same costs downstream – as the big winners did upstream – just to eliminate the competitive disadvantage caused by their failure to act now.

You are in position to be one of the big winners. All that's needed is (a) the courage to openly and honestly confront the differences between "what is" and "what should be" and then, (b) an unbending commitment to effective action needed to change "what is" to "what should be." **In your case, are these traits present or missing?**

## Deepening Your Understanding

A friend of ours once bought a brand new Harley Davidson motorcycle – the incomparable "Hog." The first thing he did was take it apart – completely – and then put it back together. We asked why.

His reply: "Because it deepened my understanding of how each part of this bike is designed to work in concert with the other parts, and how the combined effect is an overall capability that could not be achieved without careful attention to the alignment, linkage, and interdependence of these parts. I'll now be able to maximize the performance and sustainability of this bike, because I'll know how to repair or improve a part in ways that will repair and improve the whole."

This is what we're going to do for you with The Universal Purpose of Corporate Governance: Break it down into its parts, see how the Top Ten Principles of the Strategic Governance System are built into those parts, and then put it all back together again, providing you with that deep understanding needed to maximize the performance and sustainability of your whole organization. This deepened understanding of the systems level of thought and action will enable you to use the Top Ten Principles of Strategic Governance – as a system – to develop, implement, maintain, and adapt your own unique, proprietary purpose for corporate governance that aligns with The Universal Purpose, thereby creating a new and powerful sustainable competitive advantage.

Each part, which we will dissect and discuss in detail, is carefully designed to connect with the other parts to create a whole. This is an important point to keep in mind as you deepen your understanding of each component. If you feel the need to disagree with any of the material, or the need to edit or amend it, we encourage you to broaden your thinking and, instead, *think* to embrace the overall system.

## As You Read This Book…

To maximize the value of this book, we encourage you to avoid listening and thinking in these common, binary ways:

> I agree/disagree.
>
> I understand/don't understand.
>
> I like this/don't like this.
>
> This makes me feel good/bad.
>
> This makes me look good/bad.

Instead, to get the most out of this book, we recommend listening and thinking with this question always in mind:

> **What's missing for me that, if present, would enable me and our firm to perform at a level that right now seems impossible?**

It's a hard fact that there is always something *missing* that's needed to get us to the next level of effectiveness. We believe that something is in this book, available to you if you are open to receiving it.

## Develop a Deep Understanding Disassemble/Reassemble

Disassembled, here is how The Universal Purpose of Corporate Governance looks:

- Integrate
- Ethical values and standards
- Professional value and standards
- Industry values and standards
- Cultures
- Strategies
- Risk
- Stakeholders
- Sustainable world

And so we begin our analysis and discussion of each part.

## Integrate

Years ago, an academic colleague of ours described the CEO's job as an integrator: Someone who takes parts and turns them into a whole.

Confirming this view, the CEO of a publicly-traded company once told a friend, "My job is to get everybody to play nice together – and it ain't easy." Integrating parts into a whole – managing at the systems level of thought and action – is the best way to do that.

Recently, when we used the term, "system" in a business meeting, one of the attendees said, "You don't mean a computer system when you say "system", do you?" We said, "No, we don't." The attendee responded: "I didn't think so," but seemed unclear about what we do mean by "system." So let's make that clear here and now:

> **A system is a network of interdependent components working together to achieve the shared goals of the whole.**

Research shows that under the *right conditions*, the problems of commitment, alignment, motivation, and change – in others words, the CEO's challenge of integration – getting everybody to "play nice together" – tend to take care of themselves. The integrated, systems level of thought and action representing the essence of Strategic Governance will enable you to create these so-called "right conditions" by transforming *dysfunctional heaps* into *seamless wholes*.

Our academic colleague also observed that integration is hard to do and that few CEOs do it well, if at all. His assertion is confirmed by Peter Senge, author of *The Fifth Discipline*, which is Senge's term for the systems level of thought and action. In effect, Senge said integration, which he calls leadership by design, is the most difficult type of leadership and, even though most rewarding, the type of leadership most frequently ignored.

In 2009, we were discussing Strategic Governance and the systems level of thought and action at an executive committee meeting of the advisory board of The Rothman Institute of Entrepreneurship, where we serve as a board member. After listening for a while, one of our fellow board members said, with a most serious look on her face, "That kind of talk scares people." We asked why. She said, "Over lunch sometime."

In our subsequent conversation, she explained that, in her opinion, the systems level of thought and action scares people because, for most organizations, it represents large scale change; not an adjustment, not a transition, but instead, a true transformation: An order of change that cannot be made by simply telling people what to do. That would be like telling a caterpillar to perform like a butterfly without first going through the transformational process of chrysalis. Transformation scares people because it exposes them for what they don't know and can't do. And we speak from our own hard-learned experience.

In the late 1980s, we ourselves were inquiring about what was missing that, if present, would enable us to perform at a level which at that time seemed impossible. Through this inquiry, we began to see Total Quality Management (TQM) as a possibility for breakthrough and transformation, so we committed to learning more about it.

This commitment sent us on a benchmarking trip to Florida Power & Light (FP&L), the only American company to win the Deming Award, the Japanese award for quality excellence that was the inspiration for the US-based Malcolm Baldrige National Quality Award. (Catch the bitter irony of a Japanese quality award named after an American quality expert? More about that later.)

At the beginning of our meeting at FP&L, the hosting executive asked, "How can I help you?" We said, "Just start talking about your quality journey, and we'll listen." So he began. But even though he was speaking English, he was speaking a foreign language. This was both frustrating and encouraging. Frustrating because we didn't understand; encouraging because it made us wonder how differently we would think and act if we did understand.

Sensing our frustration, the FP&L executive said, "I'm not helping much, am I?" We responded: "Sure you are. We're listening for what's been *missing* that, if present, would enable us to perform at a level that right now seems impossible. You've already convinced us that TQM is missing, because we have no idea what you're talking about. Now we need to figure out if TQM is an opportunity for a breakthrough in our performance." So he kindly indulged us and kept talking, and we started to ask questions.

Finally, the breakthrough happened. "Let me put it to you this way," he said: "We pulled every FP&L employee through the keyhole called TQM, and when they came out on the other side, their work was the same, but it looked different to them, and the way they did it was completely different." We said, "Stop right there. We need to understand what that means – "pull every FP&L employee through the keyhole called TQM" – as well as you do. We sense that when we do, we'll be able to perform at a breakthrough level that right now seems impossible." And we were right.

Think back to the caterpillar/butterfly analogy. The FP&L executive effectively said he transformed their workforce from caterpillars into butterflies and then let them decide how to do their work. Can you imagine telling a caterpillar to do the work you expect from it as a butterfly *before* it becomes a butterfly? *Just tell us what you want us to do!*

And remember that quality is all about continuous improvement, the "relentless pursuit of perfection." In the mid-1990s, when we ourselves had become established quality experts, we were retained to teach quality to an American division of a German-based chemical firm. After getting to know several of the German nationals quite well, one night – shall we say sometime beyond our first beer – one of our German friends said, "You Americans talk about quality, but from the German point-of-view, you don't even know what quality is." We remembered our quality meeting at FP&L and thought, "This may be another opportunity to move to higher ground – the German view of quality – and achieve another breakthrough in our performance."

Several years later, we were asked to help transform a consumer products firm from an immature, dysfunctional heap into a mature, integrated whole. As always, we began the process with one-on-one interviews with the senior management team. In one of our update meetings with the CEO, he said, "People don't know what you're talking about." We said, "Good." He said, "WHAT? How can that be good?" We explained to the CEO, "Your people will never understand what we're talking about standing where they stand, thinking how they think, listening how they listen, acting how they act. Have you ever heard the expression, 'It's a lot easier to act yourself into a better way of thinking than it is to think yourself into a better way of acting?'" He said, "No, but I like it." We responded: "Good, because it's what we have to do here." The circle was now complete. We were now the FP&L executive, and the CEO was us. It was now *his* time to learn how to lead by design and pull his organization through the keyhole of Strategic Governance, transforming his workforce from caterpillars into butterflies.

Earlier, we said all that's needed for large scale success is (a) the courage to openly and honestly confront the differences between "what is" and "what should be" and then, (b) an unbending commitment to effective action needed to change "what is" to "what should be." At that time in the life cycle of this firm, these traits were missing in the CEO, and the transformation was aborted. *Just tell them what you want them to do!*

In summary, the first reason the systems level of thought and action scares people is that, in almost all cases, it represents the highest order of change – **transformation.** Large scale change scares people. How many caterpillars do you think would opt out of the transformational process of chrysalis if you gave them the choice: "You want me to do what? For how long? Are you nuts?" That's the difference between human beings and caterpillars: We have to choose effective change; caterpillars have it imposed upon them.

This is why we say about people underway in business transformation, "Let them scream all the way to nirvana." Because scream they will as they resist the change. And if the leaders are themselves scared, the transformation will never happen. This is why so many strategic initiatives fail: Unlike the Strategic Governance approach, they do not account for the human system of the organization, and therefore fail to transform "resistance to change" into "unbending commitment to change."

This summary gets into the second reason why our board colleague said the systems level of thought and action scares people – leaders in particular. It's because they've heard about it for years in one form or another, and most, if not all, still don't know how to do it, and therefore aren't doing it. When you're not doing what you should be doing because you don't know how, and you don't want people to find out, when someone brings the topic up, that is scary. But it's like our mothers used to say to us when we were kids: "You never should have been in that situation in the first place!"

Our solution: Follow Mom's advice and get into a better situation. How? **By mastering the Strategic Governance System**. We've made it easy for you. Follow our process, and you'll be successful.

## Dr. Deming and Continuous Improvement

By quickly reviewing the second half of the life of the late, great Dr. W. Edwards Deming, we find answers to the vital questions of "How long has this systems talk been around?" and, "How deep is the fear of and resistance to it?

Dr. Deming was introduced to Japanese statisticians and scientists in the late 1940s. He was involved in the surveying of housing, agriculture, fishing, and the population census as a member of General Douglas MacArthur's postwar occupational economic and scientific staff. In 1950, as the occupation was ending, Deming was invited back to Japan to teach methods for the achievement of quality. The fact that he was available to go is – we believe – a root cause to most, if not all, of our economic problems over the last 60 years.

While it is conventional wisdom that Deming taught the Japanese all about the statistical control of quality, that is not really the case. Consider this 1950 excerpt from Deming's personal diary: "Professor Matsuyama and his assistants will teach the statistical control of quality in the afternoons. I shall teach during the forenoons the theory of a system, and cooperation." How different would things be today if Deming had been teaching systems theory and cooperation to *Fortune 500* business leaders instead of Japanese scientists and statisticians? And how different would the mindset of those leaders have been for them to have the courage and commitment to learn and apply what Deming had to offer? The following anecdote suggests the answer.

In the late 1980s, years after Dr. Deming had become a quality icon, we heard a speaker describe an event where the CEO of a large-cap firm decided it was time to get serious about quality, so he retained the services of no one less than Deming himself to teach quality to his senior management. The CEO kicked off the meeting, saying how nothing is more important to the long-term success of the company than quality, which is why he hired Dr. Deming to teach it. He then wished the group well and left. As the CEO was walking down the hall, he heard footsteps, so he turned around to see who was following him. It was Deming: **"If you're leaving, I'm leaving."**

Dr. Deming died in 1993. In one of his obituaries, it was reported that Deming said he would like to be remembered as someone who spent his life trying to keep America from committing suicide. This life-long goal of Deming reflects the belief that failed organization are never murdered, and that they do indeed commit suicide. Assuming for the moment that Deming has been watching you from above since 1993, do you think he considers his life a failure or success?

### Was Deming Right?

Deming was right. Eli Goldratt (*The Goal*), was right. G. Bennett Stewart (*The Quest for Value*), Michael Porter (*Competitive Advantage*), Gary Hamel and C. K. Prahalad (*Competing For The Future*), Robert Keidel (*Corporate Players*), Curt Crawford

(*Compliance & Conviction*), Sir Adrian Cadbury (*The Company Chairman*), Peter Senge (*The Fifth Discipline*), Ram Charan (*What The CEO Wants You To Know*) and Jim Collins (*Good To Great*) – all of these expert commentators were right.

So were Albert Einstein, Martin Heidegger, Georg Hegel, and Peter Drucker. That's why the wisdom of all these people, plus the wisdom of unnamed others, has been built into our continuously improving management systems over the last 30 years, resulting in today's Strategic Governance System.

Sometimes the improvement was an adjustment, sometimes a transition, and sometimes, it was a trip through the keyhole of transformation. All the work has been done, and done for you. All you have to do is learn how to skillfully utilize the methods and principles of Strategic Governance. In doing so, you will transform your organization into an *integrated*, high-performance workplace, where your mostly ordinary people will consistently achieve extraordinary results.

A CEO that had the courage and commitment to create the degree of change needed to achieve the extraordinary took this action several years ago. When his staff started to come out on the far side of the keyhole of business transformation, one of them said – in front of 40 other top executives – "This system of management you are giving us removes all opportunity to fail." That's leadership, yes? Moving your staff to a level of thinking and acting where future success is a certainty, and failure a thing of the past. And by the way, in the next two years, that firm doubled in market value, and we were only working with one of two business units! That's *their* Strategic Governance story. What will *yours* be? Will Dr. Deming feel like a success or failure when he watches you from above over the next five years?

Many CEOs say they believe that people are the company's most important asset. That is and always has been a half-baked notion. When you cook it to completion, it becomes clear that the *organization* – which includes the people – is the company's most important asset. There is much more leverage in working on the organization, than there is in working on the people in that organization.

If you get the organization right, the organization will get the people right. If you don't get the organization right, you'll never be able to get the people right. It just doesn't work. It's the difference between quality control (QC) and quality assurance (QA) – huge! With QA, by controlling variability in your organization, you maximize predictability, a fundamental purpose of quality. With QC, because you don't control variability, you cannot predict outcome, so you have to stop at each stage of any process and "inspect" for quality. QC is the antithesis of the systems level of thought and action.

Understanding and managing this distinction between QC and QA at the organizational level is arguably the most important, challenging, and rewarding part of being a business leader. Moreover, as a rare, valuable, and "difficult to imitate" skill, it is a core competency and source of competitive advantage. It is the systems level of thought and action, leadership by design and, yes, it is Strategic Governance.

Hopefully, this brief review of Deming's life and work will help you better understand our academic colleague's assertion that integration is hard to do and that few CEOs do it well. Peter Senge confirmed this assertion in *The Fifth Discipline*, which again, *ala* Deming, is the systems level of thought and action, which

American leaders chose to let Deming teach to their friends in Japan rather than to them. *If you're leaving, I'm leaving.*

So, while Peter Senge was correct in saying that integration of organizational parts into a synergistic whole – leadership by design – is the most difficult type of leadership, and thus, even though most rewarding, the type of leadership most frequently ignored, we have solved that problem by making it much easier for any leader to achieve the extraordinary, if only they are willing to give Strategic Governance a try.

This is why Strategic Governance is a potential competitive advantage to you: It will enable you and your firm to perform in a way that is rare, valuable, difficult to imitate, and costly to duplicate, yet simple enough to steer and control.

The center of the Strategic Governance System's ability to create effective integration leading to extraordinary results, is culture. Culture is the social energy that drives organizational performance. When skillfully managed to create a "united nations" environment, as opposed to an environment of warring tribes, culture fulfills its purpose of coordination, adaptability, and high performance.

High-performance cultures are enabled by adaptability; adaptability is enabled by coordination; and coordination is enabled by integration. Note the linkage, as in a system!

## Ethical Values and Standards

Since this is the first of three discussions of values and standards – *ethical, professional, and industry* – we will spend some time here addressing what we mean by "values and standards."

By **values,** we mean beliefs and behaviors that establish the organization's character. Values make up a big part of culture.

By **standards**, we mean authoritative patterns for guidance to achieve excellence and correctness.

Generally, values tend to be firm-specific, and standards tend to be professional, industry, or geographic-specific.

As we increasingly become a global economy, there is a growing need for global standards, like our Universal Purpose of Corporate Governance. Standards should create a context for values, and values, when practiced, should enable the achievement of standards.

Ethical values and standards represent the threshold level and are therefore listed first in The Universal Purpose of Corporate Governance. You can be ethical without adhering to professional or industry values and standards, but you should not be able to engage in unethical behavior while adhering to such values and standards. If you can, something is wrong that needs to be fixed.

Behaving ethically means adhering to the norms for "right" conduct. It is one rung up from "legal" behavior. How often have you heard in private discussions, "We didn't break any laws", and yet a crisis ensues? If all you can say about a planned course of actions is, "It's perfectly legal," there's a good chance it's unethical and the wrong thing to do. At a National Association of Corporate Directors (NACD) Chapter meeting in New York City, one of the panelists made this point by sharing his observations of a firm as a new board member: "Nothing they were doing was illegal, but it was all wrong!"

Conventionally, ethical behavior means being open, honest, transparent, forthright, fair and equitable. In Strategic Governance, we take it to a new level by defining ethical behavior as *managing the intersection of competence and integrity.* This is a major departure from past practice and conventional wisdom.

Did the boards of all the *too-big-to-fail*, large, mid-sized and small financial services firms that contributed to our global economic crisis assure that their management teams had the *competence* needed to create organizational *integrity?* We believe the answer speaks for itself.

Did the members of these boards even recognize that assuring management possessed this competence was one of their most important responsibilities to the shareholders? How many people have been offered CEO positions by boards without having to demonstrate this essential competence – which we described earlier as integration, leadership by design and the systems level of thought and action?

By establishing this interdependent relationship between ethics, competence (of the individual), and integrity (of the organization), we position ourselves to integrate ethical values and standards with professional and industry values and standards to reflect the following Strategic Governance axiom:

> **Ethical behavior, defined as individual competence producing organizational integrity, is essential to practicing professional and industry values and standards.**

As a case in point, on the evening of April 28, 2010, after members of Congress grilled the leadership of Goldman Sachs for their questionable business practices, we overheard a conversation while commuting home on the train in which Congress was attacked for not understanding the business Goldman Sachs is in: "This is what Goldman does – they're market-makers. They make new markets offering new products to their clients. It's up to the clients if they buy or not."

Were the actions of Goldman Sachs consistent with professional and industry values and standards? Let's say yes. But Congress was coming from a different place. Congress wanted to know if these practices were *ethical* and indicative of organizational *integrity*, topics that went unaddressed by our fellow commuters that night.

Note that Goldman Sachs states that it has no plans to continue these practices. This demonstrates what Professor Mervyn King calls the "withering effect of transparency": If you want to stop an unethical practice, simply move it from a private setting to a public one, and apply a bit of patience.

## Professional Values and Standards

When creating The Universal Purpose of Corporate Governance in Dubai, the assembled group of delegates reached that satisfying point in the process when we felt we had successfully completed the job. But not everyone was content: "We missed something," one delegate declared. So others asked him what we missed. "I don't know, but something's missing." Some of the participants said, in effect, "You don't know what's missing, because nothing is – the statement is complete."

But one participant said, "No, if he [the delegate] feels something is missing, we should engage in an inquiry, together, about what that something is." And so we did.

What was missing? **Professional values and standards**. And just so you know, the same person who knew something was missing came up with the answer once the inquiry got underway. Now let's see just how much we missed.

Consider: Board Director, Chief Executive Officer, Chief Financial Officer, General Counsel, Chief Information Officer, HR Executive, Quality Manager, Chief Risk Officer, Investor Relations Officer, and Auditor. *All* these positions in organizations are responsible for keeping current with the values and standards of excellence of their profession, and then skillfully integrating these values and standards into the organizations they serve in ways that increase firm-level, long-term success.

Our team of governance experts in Dubai felt that, had this been done more consistently over the last several years, we would not have created the global economic crisis that we did.

For example, the most fundamental responsibility of the board is fiduciary: Protecting the capital investments of shareholders by making sure management does not pursue self-interest at the expense of long-term shareholder interest. Too many boards have failed to carry out this responsibility, often using the excuse that they don't want to cross the line between the role of the board and the role of management – "Noses in, fingers out", as the old saying goes.

While this "bad result plus a good excuse" approach to corporate governance has become conventional wisdom and common practice, it cannot be justified in the context of the professional board standard for performing its fiduciary responsibility.

Investors entrust their capital to the board – not management. This is important and should be posted in the boardroom. Any responsibility senior management has is delegated to them by the board. One of our valued editors, James W. Fraser, Executive Director of the National Association of Corporate Directors Research Triangle Chapter in North Carolina, said, "This is a good point, but I'll bet most people don't realize it."

The line between the role of the board and the role of management is set by the board, not management. Moreover, as governance expert Dr. Curtis Crawford has said, it is a "floating line" whose movement should be skillfully managed by the board to assure long-term value creation for their shareholders. One could easily argue that managing this floating line is the board's most important responsibility. By mastering your effective application of the Strategic Governance System, you will manage this critical issue at a level of excellence.

## Becoming a Strategic Business Partner

Another example of the importance of professional values and standards is a professional standard applicable to most of the positions we mentioned: The standard for serving as a Strategic Business Partner (**SBP**).

This is the fundamental role for all positions supporting line management. When done effectively, serving as a SBP is a highly-leveraged activity demonstrating the powerful relationship between *function* and *practice:* The relatively few members of the SBP support *functions* get paid by the shareholders to assure that the many line managers achieve excellence at the functional *practice* of their professional discipline. Let's take as examples what we call "The Big Three" of support functions: Finance, HR and IT.

Each of these disciplines is a germane dimension of line management responsibility. If you manage *capital,* you're a finance manager. If you manage *people,* you're an HR manager. And if you manage *technology,* you're an IT manager. The members of these support functions are responsible for developing empowerment tools tailored to the needs and environment of the business they support, and then transferring effectiveness in the use of those tools to line management in ways that cause line management to increase long-term shareholder value.

Unfortunately, in many companies, too few support functions play the SBP role well for several reasons. One common reason is that directors and officers of the firm don't know this role is an option. When this unawareness is present in cases where the support functions are ready, willing, and able to serve as SBPs, you have support function *push* on line management instead of what you should have: line management *pull* on support functions. Line management pull is created when the hierarchy – boards and CEOs – demand that line managers achieve excellence at practice in these functional areas by fully utilizing the capacity of these SBPs.

For example, imagine having an annual award ceremony for your firm's Finance, HR and IT "executive of the year." Members of these support functions would be excluded from consideration. Instead, they would nominate the candidates – drawn from the pool of line managers – for the CEO and board, who would then select and reward the winners. Alternatively, imagine the outcome if your firm does not do this and all of your competitors do.

When support functions play the SBP role effectively, they meet the criteria for strategic asset and sustainable competitive advantage: rare, valuable, difficult to imitate, serving as a source of superior returns through sustainable means. *Strategic Governance* is the new, breakthrough SBP standard for support functions because, by design, it enables what support functions are supposed to do: **Bring forth individual competence and organizational integrity through the systems level of thought and action in ways that assure long-term success for the firm and all of its valued stakeholders.**

## Industry Values and Standards

Before beginning our comments on the importance of industry values and standards, let's review the six assertions that serve as the foundation for The Universal Purpose of Corporate Governance:

- The four pillars of governance are government, education, professional associations, and industry. (.govs, .edus, .orgs, and .coms)
- Government needs to coordinate with education and professional associations to provide guidance and support to industry.
- Industry values and standards need to be managed by industry and trade associations in the contexts of professional and ethical values and standards toward the goal of sustainability.

- The focus should be on the creation and management of firm-level cultures based on ethical, professional, and industry values and standards.
- The goal for industry and professional values and standards is to set the bar higher than ethical values and standards and governmental regulations, whose purpose is to serve as a safety net to prevent economic fiascos like *Enronitis* beginning in 2001 and the capital market crisis beginning in 2008.
- If a firm, unit, function, or individual is not conforming with all three categories of values and standards, it is unethical to continue on that path. Governments should prevent this through regulation, legislation and enforcement.

The **third** assertion provides an excellent context in which to now address industry values and standards:

> **Industry values and standards need to be managed in the contexts of professional and ethical values and standards toward the goal of *sustainability*.**

The value of this assertion is that it provides a **common language, common ground** and **common cause** for all industries needed to create our global eco-system. The common language and common ground will come from the shared commitment to common ethical and professional values and standards. The common cause is ***sustainability.***

By this time, you should be sensing the integrity and soundness of the Strategic Governance System: **integrating interdependent parts into systematic wholes.**

We defined ethical behavior as individual competence utilized to create organizational integrity. We then integrated multiple professional disciplines into a whole using the SBP roles and responsibilities as a common language, ground and cause. Now we're unifying industries by holding them accountable for adherence to ethical and professional values and standards and the common cause of sustainability.

In doing so, together, we take a major step towards achieving The Universal Purpose of Corporate Governance: To integrate ethical, professional, and industry values and standards into firm-level cultures that enable winning strategies, manage risk, meet the needs and expectations of the firm's stakeholders, and fulfill the firm's responsibility for a sustainable world.

Finally, reflecting our systems level of thought and action, we are again revealing the interdependent relationship between ethical, professional, and industry values and standards. Meeting industry values and standards requires adherence to professional values and standards; meeting professional values and standards requires adherence to ethical values and standards; and meeting ethical values and standards means managing the competence of individuals to achieve integration leading to the integrity of organizations and broader eco-systems.

We assert that adherence and commitment to ethical and professional values and standards as a common language, common ground and common cause for all industries will have a transformational impact on the sustainability of our now global community. This assertion stands on the cumulative power of systems thinking and action: The culture that we create in the Strategic Governance System is the product of ethical values and standards times (X) professional values and standards times (X) industry values and standards.

> **Linkage equals synergy; synergy equals competitive advantage; competitive advantage equals long-term success.**

When we shift perspective from professional values and standards to industry values and standards, we shift our organizational focus *from* professional associations – such as the National Association of Corporate Directors, Financial Executives International, the National Investor Relations Institute, the National Association of Corporate Secretaries and Governance Professionals, the American Bar Association, the Society of Information Management, and the Human Capital Institute – *to* trade or industry associations such as the Chemical Manufacturers Association, Consumer Health Care Products Association, Grocery Manufacturers/Food Products Association, Pharmaceuticals Research and Manufacturers of America, National Association of Manufacturers, and the various state-specific bankers associations. Industry associations are the *customers* of professional associations, because they represent organizational *wholes* whose *parts* include the positions represented and enhanced by the professional association.

Just as a well-designed business planning process integrates the strategic plan into the operating plan – so you have one business plan – industry values and standards should integrate and reflect ethical and professional values and standards. Let's make sure they do.

As the context for the organizational level that will achieve The Universal Purpose of Corporate Governance and provide long-term success for its valued stakeholders, industry values and standards should energize organizations to increase their awareness about the overall environment. They should inspire and motivate these organizations to enrich their stakeholders and move towards the goal of a more sustainable world.

The sources of this energy are the ethical and professional values and standards. They should be integrated into the industry values and standards in ways that are tailored to the needs and environment of that industry, while concurrently serving as boundaries to ensure industry purity, wholeness and goodness:

- Is the vision for the industry pure and beneficial to the global community?
- Is the industry's purpose well-intended?
- Do industry leaders seek and speak the truth?
- Do industry leaders "walk the talk" – not merely say what they do, but actually do what they say?
- Is the industry environmentally and socially justifiable, not associated with the production of useless, harmful, or evil goods and services?
- Does the industry keep in mind its members' true nature and how they contribute to the success of our global eco-system?
- Does the industry integrate governance, strategy, risk, culture, and sustainability?

When industry values and standards meet these criteria, we have done the work needed to produce the type of culture essential to fulfilling The Universal Purpose of Corporate Governance.

## Culture

Over the years, we have created, embraced, and integrated ideas and concepts about culture that enable us to provide you with the ability to unleash the true power of your organization. By now, you should be aware that culture is the point of power exchange in the Strategic Governance System: Ethical, professional, and industry values and standards as inputs; winning strategies, managed risk, delighted stakeholders, and a sustainable world as outputs. **The center is culture**.

In one of our consulting sessions with a client, we were training and educating the executive team using an earlier version of the Strategic Governance System. Suddenly, one of the executives jumped up and proclaimed, "I just had a breakthrough! I just realized for the first time in my life that culture is not something you're stuck with, that you can use as a good excuse for not doing a great job. Culture is something we get paid to manage, so *everyone* in the company can do a great job." We were so pleased with this incident of breakthrough thinking, a journey through the keyhole of transformation.

Culture is well-defined as the *social energy* in an organization available to achieve long-term success. The opposite of culture is *entropy:* The energy drained out of the organization that could have otherwise been available for achievement. Another reinforcing definition of culture is "the patterns, beliefs and behaviors of the workforce that maximize integration, coordination, and adaptability."

All other things being equal, an integrated, coordinated, and adaptable organization has more social energy to achieve long-term success than a dysfunctional, uncoordinated, and rigid organization, whose energy is being sucked down the drain of entropy.

These definitions of culture are embedded in **Principles 7** and **9** of the Strategic Governance System. **Principle 7** states that strategy and culture are fundamental *board* responsibilities. This does not mean that strategy and culture are not fundamental *management* responsibilities. They are. Organizational effectiveness is not a game of either/or, but instead a game of and/both, of nature and degree.

It is perfectly clear to everyone that management has primary responsibility for the operation of the organization, for the implementation of strategy. At the same time, it's equally clear the board is **accountable** to the shareholders for assuring management's operation of the organization provides the level of sustainable returns shareholders expect for the risk they incur by investing in that business.

To fulfill this responsibility to the shareholders, the board must be integrally involved with management "upstream" of operations, in the highly-leveraged activities of strategy formulation and organizational design which, of course, include culture.

**Principle 9** states the essence of culture: *Adaptability*. This principle also states that culture must be derived from strategy and then leveraged to enable strategy. As we drill down deeper into this principle, we'll again reveal the interconnectivity of the parts making up the whole of the Strategic Governance System.

## Adaptability as a Strategic Asset

Great leaders know the value of adaptability – the ability to change. Producing superior *supplies* of adaptability provides firms with a greater ability to respond to the *demand* for change imposed upon them as an individual firm or part of an entire industry by uncaring, often harsh, external driving forces, which are mostly beyond their control. Your firm's superior ability to respond to the demand for change better and faster than the competition is a strategic asset, competitive advantage, and source of long-term shareholder value.

This fact leads to the conclusion that the only thing that should be structured into an organization is the ability to change: "Structured adaptability." As **Principle 9** states, adaptability is the purpose of culture, which has been similarly described as the glue that binds people together in an organization, so they function as an integrated whole instead of a dysfunctional heap; as a united nation instead of warring tribes.

An excellent example of an integrated whole with high supplies of adaptability – and the inspiration for the cover of this book – comes from nature. The Starling bird as a species has developed a remarkable ability to practice what is called "Swarming Intelligence." This intelligence is based on a high degree of awareness and exceptional reflexes. Each bird is keenly aware of the movement of the six nearest birds around it, and has the reflexes to instantly coordinate with the movements of these birds. This enables the Swarm to increase in density when attacked by a predator, and to constantly spilt and re-form into the most effective organization based on the prevailing conditions at any point in time. This high level of organizational intelligence, awareness, and agility, achieved by following a few simple rules, can be achieved in your firm by a system of well-managed support functions interacting with line management as Strategic Business Partners – a key characteristic of the professional values and standards included in The Universal Purpose of Corporate Governance.

> **Complementary, mutually reinforcing, the systems level of thought and action. This is Strategic Governance!**

Let's again take it to the next level of effectiveness. Beyond beating the competition on the field of play, there's creating a whole new field of play where the rules of competition are tailored to your firm's distinctive knowledge, skills and abilities. By managing culture to create a high-performance workplace with superior supplies of adaptability, you can now transform your firm into an external driving force that imposes change – harsh and uncaring – on your competition.

Are customer demands being met by several competitors? Convince the customer to demand more, beyond the capacity of your competition but comfortably inside your envelope of adaptability. Are industry standards for a sustainable world being met by all? Incite change to a higher level. It may be costly for your firm to adapt, but not as costly as for the competition. Tell shareholders they should expect higher returns than they've been getting from the sector in which you compete. Again, this may be disruptive to your firm as part of that sector, but with your superior supply of adaptability, you will be able to adjust in less time, at less expense, and with a better outcome than the competition.

This demonstrates how **culture management** and the aggressive use of **adaptability** are used to increase the heat that drives your competition out of the kitchen.

## Culture/Strategy

This aggressive exploitation of adaptability is an important aspect of the interdependent relationship between culture and strategy, which follows next in our statement of The Universal Purpose of Corporate Governance.

The dynamic between culture and strategy is highly nuanced, embedded with multiple distinctions. Each distinction you master, each nuance you embrace, serves as a new empowerment tool for achieving the extraordinary. The key is to develop these tools and begin using them better and faster than your competition.

At the most fundamental level, strategy answers the question, "What should we do?", and culture answers the question, "How are we going to behave when we do it?" When managed effectively, the "how" of culture enables the "what" of strategy. This applies both to strategy formulation and strategy implementation. But the interdependence between culture and strategy runs even deeper.

**Principle 2** states the essence of strategy is sustainable competitive advantage, and that its purpose is to create an integrated and coordinated set of commitments and actions designed to develop strategic assets and then leverage those assets to create sustainable competitive advantages and long-term shareholder value. We hope you hear the purpose of culture embedded in this purpose of strategy: "integrated," "coordinated," "commitments," and "actions." This leads us to the distinctions between different types of strategic assets and how they form a powerful system of competitive advantage.

In the Strategic Governance System, we have created four types of strategic assets, each enabling the other: Leadership, Organization,

Process, Products/Services. Looking back now over the past 25 years, recall that we used to benchmark *products and services*. Then we started to benchmark the *processes* that produced those products and services. This led to the "best practices" line of thought, which it seems people still adhere to in spite of the research indicating that simply copying another firm's so-called "best practice" will invariably produce disappointing results.

Here's why: Benchmarking processes is analogous to benchmarking one part of a multi-part product. Not a total waste of time, but certainly not optimal. Processes are parts of organizational wholes, and focusing on these parts without also focusing on the whole is a competitive *dis*advantage.

We strongly discourage the practice. At the same time, before an organization can become a *whole,* the right type of leadership must be present. Too often, this type of leadership is missing, which is why, perhaps, so many people are stuck at the "best practices" level.

The type of leadership we are referring to is *leadership by design*, also described as *leadership by architecture*. This is different from other leadership types such as *leadership by example*, or *leadership by collaboration*.

## Leadership by Design

Leadership by design means working *on* the business to enhance the performance of the people working *in* the business. Leadership by design means building and managing the organizational equivalent of the human central nervous system to create "smart" organizations, where ordinary people achieve extraordinary results. The Strategic Governance System is the tool kit for building these smart organizations.

The product of leadership by design is an organizational whole, where all the parts are aligned, linked, and working interdependently to create a state of *positive synergy,* where 1+1+1 = >3. When leadership by design is missing, instead of integrated wholes, organizations are dysfunctional heaps, where 1+1+1 = < 3. In these "dumb" organizations, smart people have to make extraordinary efforts to produce ordinary results.

Unlike dumb organizations, smart organizations are great places to work. The environment of organizational intelligence enables these firms to attract, retain, and develop great workforces. Inspired and motivated by working in smart organizations where they can achieve the extraordinary, these great workforces put forth extra, discretionary effort to deliver great value to the customers in ways that deliver great value to the shareholders. Strategy, culture, structure, and systems are aligned, so it becomes clear what knowledge, skills and abilities the workforce should have. The effect is an organization with staff that has the skills and styles to manage the systems, in the structure, to practice the culture, in ways that achieve the strategy.

This high-performance workplace environment breeds the enduring *behavioral* core competencies that cause your organization and workforce to be sources of sustainable competitive advantages. (Think of models of consistent high-performance achievements, such as emergency hospital rooms, aircraft carrier deck operations crews, police SWAT teams, and spacecraft launch management teams.)

In the context of this system of strategic assets – leadership enabling organization, organization enabling process, process enabling products and services – let's disassemble and then reassemble the Strategic Governance definition of Strategy to achieve our goal of deep understanding needed for mastery and extraordinary results.

In doing so, we will draw on the principles of Strategic Governance, to varying degrees, demonstrating how they are all interdependent, forming a system.

## Principle 2
## The Essence of Strategy

Assembled:

An *integrated* and *coordinated* set of *commitments* and *actions designed* to first develop *strategic assets* and then *leverage* those strategic assets to create *sustainable competitive advantage* and *long-term shareholder value.*

Disassembled:
- Integrated and Coordinated
- Commitments
- Actions
- Design
- Strategic Assets
- Leverage
- Sustainable Competitive Advantage
- Long-term Shareholder Value

## Integrated and Coordinated

The value and purpose of having integration and coordination present has been covered in our discussion of culture **(Principles 9** and **10)**, which led seamlessly into this discussion of strategy, as it should. The causal relationship between integration, coordination and adaptability brings forth an important distinction between two levels of strategy tied to our strategic asset system of leadership, organization, process, and product/services. The first level is focused on leadership and organization as strategic assets. The second leverages the leadership and organizational capabilities of the first to develop process and product/services into strategic assets. In other words, when applying the definition of Strategy, do so at all four levels: Leadership, Organization, Process, and Products/Services.

Integration and coordination are in effect the essences of governance. (**Principle 1**) When the interests and efforts of the stakeholders have been aligned through integration and coordination, these unified forces can easily set the strategic direction of the business in terms of vision, set the bar for performance standards, and assure upstream that a sustainable world is a business priority reflected in all of the firm's decisions and actions.

## Commitments

This is a powerful tool in the Strategic Governance System, which includes methods and techniques to maximize the degree of commitment to the point where it becomes *unbending*. The system also includes change management techniques designed to transform "resistance to change" into "unbending commitment to change." An unbending commitment is when you promise to achieve a result and people count on it as if it's already done. Unbending commitments create a high performance culture of "no excuses," where "results" does not equal "no results plus a good excuse." In this culture of commitment, excuses are viewed as the problems managers get paid to solve to clear a path leading to the result of long-term shareholder value. In a culture of unbending commitment, problems get *solved* – not *admired*.

## Actions

Only actions produce results. Actions are the purpose of conversations of commitment. The positive synergy achieved in **Principle 1** by aligning the interests and efforts of stakeholders inspires and motivates those stakeholders to set aggressive, strategic directions and breakthrough performance standards. When promises of action are made with an unbending commitment to results – no excuses – these actions are highly effective, leading to extraordinary results. The effect is the elimination of errors of omission and commission. These are the two categories of errors, especially the former, that caused the painful and humiliating event we are calling the global economic crisis. Alignment of interests and efforts? Unbending commitment? Promises of results? No excuses? Hardly!

By practicing conversations of actions and unbending commitment to change, instead of conversations of knowledge and resistance to change, you preempt the concern many organizations have with the so-called "Knowing/Doing Dilemma": Why Do Smart People Often Do Dumb Things?" (It's because they confuse *sounding* smart with *doing* smart!)

## Design

Design means shaping work into a form that, when done, creates strategic assets, sustainable competitive advantage, and long-term shareholder value. The set of commitments and actions designed by directors and officers should fit into our four categories of strategic assets/core competencies: Leadership, organization, process, and products/services.

Competitors envious of your success will probably continue to benchmark your products, services, and processes, while the root cause of your success will stem from your principle-based and systematic approach to organizational design and leadership. This makes your competitive advantage difficult to imitate and, as a result, sustainable.

> **This is Strategic Governance:**
> **Organizational Alignment**
> **X**
> **Sustainable Competitive Advantage**
> **= Long-Term Success.**

## Strategic Assets

Strategic Assets are core competencies that are scalable to the enterprise level. Leadership and organizational design are examples. Because of the leverage inherent in the board role, a board of directors that meets the criteria for core competency is another example. A rare and valuable source of raw material difficult to imitate and costly to duplicate used for one of many products is not an example of a strategic asset because, while it provides a sustainable competitive advantage and is a core competency, it is not transferable to other products or areas of the business, and thus, not scalable. Strategic assets are a subset of core competencies.

"Core competencies" are *not* products, services or processes that represent the central part of your business. Instead, core competencies are resources and capabilities that are:

- Rare
- Valuable
- Difficult to imitate
- Costly to duplicate
- Controllable

> **When skillfully exploited, core competencies and strategic assets produce sustainable competitive advantage and long-term shareholder value. Moreover, the capacity of the entire organization to produce sustainable competitive advantage and long-term shareholder value is limited to the capacity and utilization of the firm's core competencies and strategic assets. The Strategic Governance System enables you to maximize the capacity of your core competencies and strategic assets, and thereby maximize your sustainable competitive advantages and long-term shareholder value.**

The most enduring categories of core competencies are, experience and research tells us, **behavioral** in nature – leadership and organizational. A company may market and sell a product that is far superior to any competitive offering or potential substitute. That product could be the result of an acquisition, as when Pfizer bought all of Warner-Lambert to get one product – the drug Lipitor® – from just one division – Parke-Davis.

Conversely, that product could come from an innovative organizational culture created by visionary leaders like Livio DeSimone, former Chairman and CEO of 3M, where they live *in* the question, "What's missing that, if present, would enable us to achieve what conventional wisdom says is impossible?"

The Pfizer approach would seem to provide a less sustainable competitive advantage over the long run than the 3M approach, because the root cause of the Pfizer advantage does not go down as deep into the Strategic Governance System of Core Competencies as the 3M advantage. Pfizer operated at the product level whereas 3M operated at the leadership level.

Moreover, if leadership and organization are not key sources of sustainable competitive advantage, the return on investment in an acquisition will be less than when leadership and organization are.

As mentioned earlier, thinking you can copy what another successful firm is doing at the product or process level and get the same result through benchmarking of best practices is not realistic. This rarely if ever happens, because the leaders of those successful firms generally perform diagnostic work and then implement organizational changes tailored to their needs and environment. The processes in these firms produce world-class products because they function as aligned, integrated and coordinated parts of a larger, organizational *whole*.

To be most effective, benchmarking should first be done at the leadership and organizational level.

When benchmarking for leadership as a core competency, we suggest the following questions:
- What leadership capabilities are used to:
    - Create, not predict, the future?
    - Lead from the top, not the front?

- Work *on* the organization to enhance the performance of the people working *in* the organization?

When benchmarking for organization as a core competency, the following questions are suggested:

- What happens when people use the organizational system the leaders designed?
- How does the organizational system create the opportunity for the workforce to behave as a sustainable competitive advantage?
- What organizational traits are used to preempt, not just compete with, the competition?
- How and why does this organization enable ordinary people to achieve extraordinary results?

This aspect of strategy – core competencies and strategic assets – is so important to long-term success that we will now cover it again from a different although reinforcing perspective.

## Strategy – Little "S" and Big "S" Distinction

In the quality discipline, a distinction is made between "Little Q" and "Big Q." Little Q is the application of quality tools and techniques – graphs, pareto charts, histograms, control charts, problem statements, targets, etc. – to the processes used to produce the products and/or services the firm sells to its customers. Big Q is the application of those same tools and techniques to *all* the processes in the firm.

Little Q is Quality Assurance. Big Q is Total Quality Management. Big Q creates a quality environment throughout the firm that enhances the performance and outcome of Little Q.

In both cases, the fundamental goals are the same – The Three Zeros: Zero defects (Six Sigma), zero lead-time, and zero variability.

We propose a similar distinction be made in strategy between Little S and Big S. Little S is the firm's plan to design, develop, market, sell, make and deliver a specific combination of products and/or services to a specific market for as long as that strategy produces results that meet and exceed the expectations of the firm's stakeholders. Big S is the ongoing development and continuous improvement of the organization's ability to formulate, implement and modify winning strategies.

In the context of Big S, the firm is the product. Big S is working *on* the business; Little S is working *in* the business. Big S enables Little S, just as Big Q enables Little Q. In the context of the Strategic Governance System of Core Competencies, Little S and Little Q are primarily focused on products and services, while Big S and Big Q are primarily focused on Organization.

The common ground is Leadership (deciding what to do) and Process (how it will get done).

To illustrate the difference between Big S and Little S, let's consider the approach two high profile CEOs took in saving their companies from demise: Don Petersen of Ford and Lee Iacocca of Chrysler. Petersen took the Big S approach, orchestrating so much pressure for change, on so many fronts, that Ford became, from the view of employees and outsiders, "a different company tapping the collective genius of the organization to identify and solve problems." Iacocca's approach, while effective, was at the Little S level, focused on products, styling, and market segments. While Iacocca saved Chrysler in that era, few if any talked about how he changed the way Chrysler functioned, as Petersen did at Ford.

Here's a checklist for doing Big S work we provided to the leader of a *Fortune 500* firm to enable the creation of a world-class organization through transformational change:

- Make sure all the pieces fit together
- Clearly and consistently signal what to do and how to behave in doing it
- Build the right degree of integration, coordination, flexibility, and strategic agility
- Balance business unit (BU) separation and integration to exploit synergies between the BUs
- Build and strengthen the corporate level competitive advantage
- Prevent duplication of effort and unhealthy internal competition and conflict
- Make sure the BUs are on track financially, strategically, and culturally

- Define the purpose and performance standards of any corporate function, focusing on the customers of each.

This Big S leadership effort caused management to "act itself into a better way of thinking" about strategy, pursuing – for the first time in the firm's history – a long-term, ongoing strategy to build and then continuously improve an organization capable of consistently beating the competition, regardless of the prevailing conditions at any point in time.

This important shift in thinking and action provided leadership with the opportunity to transform the organizational culture and achieve a major breakthrough, demonstrating the power of the Strategic Governance System of Core Competencies:

> **Leadership enabling organization, organization enabling process, and process enabling products/services.**

## Leverage

As the ancient saying goes, if you give people a big enough lever, they can move the world. Strategic assets are big levers, but they only fulfill their potential if they are effectively utilized. The entire firm's capability to achieve sustainable competitive advantage is equal to the utilized capacity of the strategic assets and core competencies of that firm. By managing the Strategic Governance System of leadership, organization, process and products/services, you will maximize this capacity and achieve the extraordinary.

> **Strategic Governance is a highly-leveraged leadership opportunity.**

## Sustainable Competitive Advantage (SCA)

The essence of strategy is SCA. Consistent with Strategic Governance **Principles 1** and **4,** SCA is enabled first, by the alignment created by governance, and then, by the core competencies and strategic assets developed through formulation and implementation of strategy.

When superior returns – the advantage – is achieved through sustainable means – core competencies and strategic assets – SCA is achieved.

## Long-term Shareholder Value

SCA greater than the returns produced by alternative investments of comparable risk is long-term shareholder value. The value is the superior return; the long-term nature of that value is derived from the sustainable means used to achieve it: core competencies and/or strategic assets.

## Principle 7
## The Relationship Between Boards, Strategy and Culture

**Principle 7** states that strategy and culture are fundamental board responsibilities. In practice, it is far from easy to involve all board members *usefully* in a discussion of strategy. This requires an imaginative effort by both the chairman and chief executive to present strategic issues to board members early enough in the process for them to have a real influence over the outcome, and in a form that encourages them to contribute positively to the development of the final strategy, which includes organizational design and culture. According to governance expert Jim Fraser, "This is where a board with diverse functional and industry experience can be most useful. A board with all sole industry experience can easily fall into a *Groupthink* mode (See Sidebar), possibly disastrous to strategy."

**Groupthink**

The antithesis of being open to new ways of thinking and acting is "groupthink". Groupthink practices are the weeds in the gardens of organizational culture and values. Tony Khuri, professor of management at Case Western in Cleveland, warns of eight types of groupthink:

1. Illusion of Invulnerability: "We all know we wouldn't release anything that isn't one hundred percent effective, right?"

2. Belief in Group Morality: "I'm not going to call for a vote because I think we're more or less in agreement here."

3. Rationalization: "I had a few concerns, but since everybody else seemed committed, in the interests of time, I didn't bother to bring them up."

4. Shared Stereotypes: "Our approach to business has worked for us in the past; odds are it will work again."

5. Self-Censorship: "Those doomsayers in legal all have an ax to grind. Why let a bunch of *nervous nellies* determine our marketing strategy?"

6. Direct Pressure: "Hey, if we don't release soon, there are going to be cutbacks, even here at this table. So, are you on board or not?"

7. Mind Guards: "What have we got to worry about? This new product is another winner."

8. Illusion of Unanimity: "No need for you to be at the meeting; I'll summarize your concerns for the board, okay?"

The strategy formulation process must be iterative, both top down and bottom up, and collaborative in nature. Strategic Governance, especially the Service and Software, represents this imaginative effort that enables your organization to achieve excellence at this highly-leveraged activity.

This concludes our detailed discussion of the parts of the system that make up Strategy. We discussed Integrated and Coordinated, Commitments, Actions, Design, Strategic Assets, Sustainable Competitive Advantage, and Long-term Shareholder Value. Assembled, these parts make up the second of our Top Ten Principles of Strategic Governance – *The Essence of Strategy:*

The essence of strategy is sustainable competitive advantage. The purpose of strategy is to create an integrated and coordinated set of commitments and actions designed to develop strategic assets and then leverage those assets to create sustainable competitive advantages and long-term shareholder. This is a primary responsibility of both the board and management.

We will now resume our discussion on the key components of The Universal Purpose of Corporate Governance, picking up with Risk, the focus of our third Top Ten Principle.

# Principle 3
# The Essence of Risk

In the early 1990s, we worked at a privately-owned company as a member of an executive team that operated as the Office of the CEO. Collectively, the executives on this team had full income and asset management responsibility for the business.

On a regular basis, our board would make this point very clear to us:

*Our job as the board of directors is to make sure you as management provide the shareholders with a superior return through sustainable means compared to returns being produced by alternative investments of comparable risk. If you can't do that, we will either replace you with a management team that can, or advise the shareholders to pull their capital from this investment and reinvest in one of those alternative investments of comparable risk that is producing a superior, sustainable return.*

This story creates an effective context for our discussion on risk by tightly linking risk to strategy, consistent with Strategic Governance **Principle 4**: Governance encompasses strategy, and strategy encompasses risk.

Today, risk needs to be put back in context. For whatever reason, too many of have been treating *strategy* and *risk* as if they are two separate and equal independent topics. This is known as a *categorical mistake*, like treating a county as if it's the same as a state, or an arm as if it's the same as a whole person.

This mistake becomes obvious when you consider the essence of strategy – SCA: Superior returns through sustainable means compared to alternative investments of comparable ***risk.***

Managing the enterprise's risk profile so that it remains in that group of alternative investments the shareholders considered when making their investment decision, and then managing the performance of that firm to outperform those alternative investments of comparable risk, is the purpose of strategy. A strategy that does not address risk management is simply incomplete.

Over the last few years, we have heard numerous presentations on risk. In these presentations, we learned about different types of risk: *Financial, strategic, asset, organizational, compliance, reputational*, and so on. But what we didn't hear is the essence of risk captured in Strategic Governance **Principle 3**:

> **Fundamentally, risk is an investor's uncertainty about the gains or losses that will result from a particular investment.**

The Strategic Governance principle of risk – and this is critically important – ties into the board's fundamental role as a governance mechanism utilized by shareholders to prevent managerial opportunism at the expense of those shareholders. With our definition of risk, the single most important board duty once again becomes clear and obvious: Make sure management does not do anything that has an adverse effect on the expected degree of uncertainty inherent in the investment, and make sure management does do things that will have a positive effect on that same degree of uncertainty.

Our concern about making so many *distinctions* about different types of risk is that these valid and useful distinctions can easily deteriorate into *distractions* from the essence of risk (**Principle 3**), causing companies like AIG to do things that can only be described as insane: selling insurance policies without prudent levels of capital reserves.

## "Too Big To Fail": Past and Present Meanings

Earlier in this book, we used the term, "too big to fail." This is an old term whose meaning has changed since the economic crisis of 2008. Analyzing how and why this change happened provides insight into effective risk management.

Before 2008, "too big to fail" was a term used by money managers to help their clients understand the difference between investing in large-cap companies and investing in mid or small-cap companies. The former, due to their critical mass, were more conservative, lower-risk equity investments because they were "too big to fail." The latter were considered more aggressive, higher-risk investments because they were not "too big to fail."

Another way to state this: Conventional wisdom was that the large-cap companies were able to absorb the adverse consequences of a bad business decision to a greater degree than smaller companies. While the upside potential of a large-cap investment was typically less than that of a mid or small-cap investment, the downside risk was also less. If preservation of principal was an important investment criterion, responsible money managers would recommend large-cap investments over mid or small-cap investments because the large-caps were simply "too big to fail." In addition, there was a prevailing assumption that these large-cap firms would likely not fail because they were ethically, professionally, and reasonably managed.

Post 2008, this is not what "too big to fail" means. Since the economic meltdown and subsequent bank bailouts of that year, "too big to fail" now means that the failure of one large firm on the global economy would be "too severe to endure." So today, for various reasons, large-cap firms are no longer considered "too big to fail" based on the historical meaning of this term, but rather by the economic and social need for them to be bailed out by the federal government if and when they would otherwise fail. This phenomenon was caused by an undisciplined approach to risk management that can be demonstrated through analysis of another popular term: "Risk appetite."

We now consistently hear that boards and management need to determine their "appetite for risk." That's fine, as long as these business leaders know that, to a large degree, in the absence of shareholder approval for a changed approach, that firm's risk appetite is a given. The better question is whether or not their management systems enable them to operate that company inside the confines of their risk profile, so they "eat" no more and no less risk than they have committed to their shareholders.

**In brief, the risk appetite of the board and management should be, to a large degree, a function of the risk appetite of their shareholders.**

Consider an analogy: A boxer has committed to fight at a certain weight. As long as that commitment remains, how much food he consumes is a matter of discipline – not discussion. He should eat enough to be at or near his promised weight, but never more. So it is with business leaders and their risk appetite. Equity investors select companies for investments from pools of alternative investments of comparable risk, based on *their* appetite for risk. Wealth is created by management for these shareholders when *operating income* exceeds the *weighted cost of capital*. This cost of capital is determined in part by a company's risk premium, or beta: That firm's volatility compared to the overall volatility of the equity market.

Ethical boards and executives should manage the business within the confines of that disclosed beta, so the portions of risk they serve to their shareholders are not greater than the risk appetite of those shareholders. And, therefore, if business leaders decide to take greater or lesser risk, they should disclose that fact to the shareholders. For example, when funded by debt, mergers and acquisitions can increase the investment risk in firms beyond the level indicated by their disclosed betas. Shareholders deserve the right to decide if they want to continue owning these investments before capital structures are leveraged and risk profiles are correspondingly altered.

For the same reason, firms should disclose decisions like those made by AIG when they decided to sell derivatives that, in effect, were insurance policies without capital reserves. Surely, by implementing this decision, AIG's leaders pushed the firm further out on the risk curve than their beta warranted, thereby "super-sizing" their shareholders with risk; all without disclosure; all without approval. In doing so, AIG showed the world how a "too big to fail" firm can – in the absence of a bailout – fail: Overindulge in risk, behaving no differently than an undisciplined middle-weight showing up at the pre-fight weigh-in exceeding the 160 pound limit. Losers in both cases!

The purpose of the Strategic Governance System is to provide business leaders – boards, CEOs, and senior management – with the tools to determine and manage their firm's risk appetite through a principle-based approach that reduces variability and increases predictability throughout the organization. This principle-based system enables business leaders to manage the organization within the boundaries of its disclosed risk profile in ways that outperform all alternative investments of comparable risk.

When you apply ethics, competency and integrity to risk management, all towards the goal of organizational soundness, you will manage risk as an integral part of a larger whole, revealing its true essence. This systems level experience is not unlike working a crossword puzzle. Yes, "automobile" is a "four-wheel, transportation vehicle that runs on gas and oil." But if there are only three spaces in the puzzle, and the letters "c", "a" and "r" are needed to complete other words, we should know which term to use, yes?

> **So it is with Risk and the Strategic Governance System:**
>
> **The essence of its role as a part of the system is to contribute to the positive synergy and high-performance capability of the whole. The Strategic Governance definition (Principle 3) does that while embracing the more micro definitions as enablers of effective risk management.**

When managed this way, as part of a system, the risk function is well positioned to serve effectively as a **Strategic Business Partner**. The essence of being a SBP is to enable the *whole* business to run better than it would without your support. The more mature the function, the more value it creates as a SBP.

By maturity, we mean integration with the other parts of the business. On the low end of the continuum, there is no risk function: "We don't manage risk, have no clue what our risks are, so we have tons of well-capitalized insurance." The next level of maturity is often called ***Administrative,*** where there is little to no integration with the rest of the business: "We have a risk manager. It's his/her job to manage risk; we have our own jobs to do."

The third level of maturity is called ***Functional***. This is when the Risk Manager develops an Enterprise Risk Management (ERM) Plan – separate from the business plan – that requires participation from all areas of the business. At a large number of companies today, this plan might be found in a binder sitting on a credenza; seldom read, unfortunately, until something happens.

And finally we come to the highest degree of risk maturity – **Integrative:** When risk is practiced daily by all managers as one of several germane dimensions of their daily work. This is how risk is managed in the Strategic Governance System.

Everything just said about risk management applies to all other support functions: **Finance, IT, HR, Quality,** and **Legal**. When all these support functions embrace and practice the Strategic Governance standard for performing as a SBP, as previously discussed, it creates a common language, common ground, and common cause among these functions, thereby enhancing their collective ability to transform the entire enterprise into a high-performance eco-system: Intelligent, integrated, coordinated, adaptable – and therefore – sustainability.

## Stakeholders

There are three primary stakeholders to consider in the context of our discussion: employees, customers and the firm's owners. Using the Strategic Governance methodology, you can choose to develop your organization into a great place to work. In doing so, you will create the organizational resources for meeting the needs and expectations of your *employee* stakeholders. This organizational capability will enable you to attract and retain skilled and motivated employees, meeting the standard for a great workforce. Under your direction, this great workforce will deliver superior value to your *customer* stakeholders, making your firm a great place to buy, increasing market share and revenues. As a great place to work, with a great workforce delivering superior value to your customers as a great place to buy, your firm will be well positioned to be a great place to invest, meeting the needs and expectations of your *owner* stakeholders.

In addition to these three primary stakeholders – employees, customers, and owners – other stakeholders include your firm's business partners, suppliers, strategic alliances, governmental and regulatory agencies and – very importantly – local communities.

## A More Sustainable World

At the end of the 2009 Middle East Governance Congress, the global cadre of board members and governance experts expressed concern that US-based attempts to solve the problems that caused the global meltdown would fail to account for the vital importance of a *sustainable world*.

They asked us – as chairman of the congress – to make sure that did not happen, saying, "In time, we'll get out of this economic mess we're in. But we're not nearly as confident that we'll be able to fix the problems of our planet. Please don't allow that aspect of the problem to be ignored when you return home to the United States."

Fast forward a few months. While having breakfast with other speakers at a financial executives roundtable session in the US, a senior financial executive and corporate director expressed his views on this topic using language as offensive as his position: "Frankly, I couldn't give a flying ___ about corporate social responsibility (CSR)." We could only imagine what our global brothers and sisters in governance and sustainability would think had they heard this.

What makes this executive's position all the more indefensible is that you need to care about CSR and creating a more sustainable world even if your concern begins and ends with long-term shareholder value, simply because so many of your current and prospective employees, customers, and investors – your primary stakeholders – *do care* about CSR and sustainability.

Contrast this one American executive's point of view on CSR to that of another: Ralph Schonenbach, CEO of global sourcing advisory firm, Trestle Group. Ralph firmly believes that financial, environmental, and social sustainability need to be integrated into the firm's culture, strategy, and governance approach. According to Ralph, "Trestle Group's commitment to social responsibility has become an integral part of our culture. This commitment is supported through a governance structure that reflects our core value of creating a more sustainable world."

Ralph's business strategy and operations reflect his words. Through his Trestle Group Foundation, Ralph and his team create sustainable economic opportunities for women-led businesses in emerging markets, in turn improving the quality of life in those societies. With the support of companies like PepsiCo Europe, IBM, and Mircrosoft, Trestle Group has supported women entrepreneurs in Bangladesh, Czech Republic, Egypt, Hungary, Uganda, and several others countries, all towards the goal of sustainability.

In a 2010 Harvard Business Review article on this topic, sustainability was described as an "inescapable strategic imperative." The article added that such strategic imperatives are the products of business megatrends, citing the quality and IT movements, electrification, and mass-production as megatrend examples.

Strategic imperatives stemming from megatrends always represent a level of performance conventional wisdom says is impossible; a level of performance beyond business as usual; a level of performance that cannot be predicted by anything done in the past. In other words, a breakthrough.

For example, the quality movement produced the imperative of error-free work and continuous improvement: Doing the right thing, the right way, the first time, and better the next time. Why? Because the principles, methods, and tools of the quality movement made this work standard possible.

This reminds us of a speaker at a conference during the early stages of the quality movement who asked the audience to answer, "True or false", to the following statement: "We all do error-free work." Everyone in the audience answered, "False." The speaker's response? "The correct answer is true. Everyone does error-free work. The problem is, we just don't do it for very long."

The ability to achieve the strategic imperative of error-free work and continuous improvement produced by the quality movement was enhanced by the IT megatrend, which also gave us the imperative of entity and procedural interdependence: Organizations functioning as intelligent systems, not unlike the human beings that make up these organizations.

Achieving this IT imperative has been hindered by the absence of the systems level of thought and action, which is now provided to the global business community by the Strategic Governance movement, all in the name of continuous improvement, evidencing our nearly 25 years of experience in the quality discipline, as well as how one movement can enable another.

As a strategic imperative, sustainability is well-defined as "utilizing resources to achieve your current organizational goals and objectives in ways that strengthen, enrich and enhance those resources, so they are available to the next generation of users in a form that enables the achievement of more advanced goals and objectives." Achieving this sustainability imperative is made possible by Strategic Governance:

- A reorientation of the individual and global business community to account for the existence of a systematic, principle-based approach to financial, social, and environmental sustainability
- Synthesis of ethical, professional, and industry values and standards
- Integration of governance with strategy, risk, culture, performance, and social responsibility
- Organizational intelligence linking strategy, organization, and operations.

Now that the Strategic Governance movement has made sustainability a realistic possible, sustainability will truly become an "inescapable strategic imperative." Why? Same as with the quality movement: The principles, methods, and tools of Strategic Governance make this sustainability standard possible. Think of it this way: The Strategic Governance movement is to sustainability as the quality movement is to error-free work and continuous improvement. Just as the quality and IT megatrends raised the bar on work standards and organizational intelligence, Strategic Governance has raised the bar on sustainability.

Strategic Governance provides the tools needed to account for the increasing concern for the social and environmental impact of a business in addition to the financial impact. Consider the exploding interest among investors in "ESG". ESG = environmental, social issues and corporate governance Key Performance Indicators (KPI) necessary to achieve sustainability. Investors are factoring in these KPIs in their decision-making – in the process making them very tangible and financial metrics.

In the planning segment of Strategic Governance, these types of issues are called **External Driving Forces,** which are the forces influencing the ability to create shareholder value in a particular sector. If you don't take them into account, adjusting your strategy, organization, and operations accordingly, your organization is not behaving intelligently, which means you are not governing strategically.

When environmental and social concerns ("E" and "S") are identified as threats and risks to the financial success of a firm, there is a powerful incentive to identify the strategic imperatives – error-free work, organizational intelligence and, sustainability – that must be carried out to cope with these driving forces. This is enabled by Strategic Governance. ("G")

Moreover, we all know by now that coping with external driving forces is needed to *survive*. To *flourish*, you must learn how to turn these driving forces into sources of advantage so that your bottom line is blacker and more stable than it would have been had you not become a global model of financial, environmental, and social sustainability.

While presenting and interacting with a large group of board directors in 2009 – several from Fortune 100 firms – one of the directors said, "These are delicate times calling for a new world order." It has also been said that, in this new world order, sustainability must become systematized and integrated into the strategy, organization, and daily operations of all firms, large and small. Those who use the Strategic Governance System to carry out this and all other strategic imperatives will have a serious competitive advantage over those who don't.

> **Out of adversity create opportunity, always in the context of assuring long-term shareholder value. That's true sustainability for investors and stakeholders.**

# SUMMARY

As our CEO colleague observed, the job of directing and managing the large corporate enterprises at the heart of the global capital markets "ain't easy." We believe that the systems approach set out in this slim volume will help you to radically and fundamentally think through the parts and whole of your own organization to make it more competitive and more sustainable over the long-term. It's our passion to spread the word on the importance of Strategic Governance, so that more corporate boards and executives are prepared to meet the significant challenges that face them in the global economy, especially in troubled times.

Remember our Harley-Davidson Zen master who disassembled and then reassembled his new toy to deepen his understanding of how this bike works, thereby helping him get maximum performance for as long as possible?

As promised, this is what we did together with **The Universal Purpose of Corporate Governance**: We broke it down into its pieces, explained how the Principles of Strategic Governance are built into those parts and how those parts are highly interdependent and synergistic. Now, we can put it all back together again, empowering you with a much deeper understanding needed for mastery of the principles.

This will allow you to use the principles to develop, implement, maintain, and adapt your own unique purpose for corporate governance that aligns with The Universal Purpose, producing a new and powerful sustainable competitive advantage for you and your firm.

Assembled:

> "**The Universal Purpose of Corporate Governance is to** *integrate ethical, professional,* **and** *industry values* **and** *standards* **into firm-level** *cultures* **that enable winning** *strategies,* **manage** *risk,* **meet the needs and expectations of the firms'** *stakeholders,* **and fulfill the firms' responsibility for a** *sustainable world.*"

# THE TOP TEN PRINCIPLES OF STRATEGIC GOVERNANCE

## Principle 1: The Essence of Governance

The essence of governance is alignment. This essence is reflected in its purpose: Align the interests and efforts of stakeholders, establish the firm's strategic direction, assure effective performance of the business, and enable a sustainable eco-system.

Governance as a function is still very much in its infancy. That does not mean it has not been around a long time. It means governance has yet to grow up, as in the old saying, "You're only young once, but you can be immature forever." The governance function is immature. One reason for this immaturity is that, until now, there has not been a principle-based, systemic approach to governance.

In the maturity cycle of a business function, there are three stages:

**Classification, Correlation, and Cause-Effect**

When people fail to define a function, or when people define it to suit their own needs, that function is not even *classified* as a recognized body of knowledge. In too many situations, this is still the case with governance.

In 2006, we observed a panel discussion debating whether or not there is any *correlation* between good governance and long-term shareholder value. Really! It is difficult if not impossible to have a quality discussion regarding correlation if the body of knowledge – in this case governance – has not been clearly and consistently classified.

Fortunately, because of the all-encompassing scope of the Strategic Governance System, it includes performance features and characteristics of more mature functions already proven to have a cause-effect relationship with sustainable competitive advantage and long-term shareholder value. But an important role for governance still exists: **Managing the business as a system.**

The key to the success of any business system is alignment of its parts. If governance can accomplish this, the other parts of the system can be that much more productive in achieving shared interests, goals, and objectives.

With the creation of Strategic Governance, the governance function can now mature into a science: A body of knowledge based on a system of principles proven to "cause the effect" of sustained success in a large range of business conditions.

## Principle 2: The Essence of Strategy

The essence of strategy is sustainable competitive advantage.

Since the topic of strategy has already been discussed in detail, we will simply restate its full purpose here:

> **The purpose of strategy is to create an integrated and coordinated set of commitments and actions designed to develop strategic assets and then leverage those assets to create sustainable competitive advantages and long-term shareholder value.**

## Principle 3: The Essence of Risk

Similar to strategy, risk was also thoroughly discussed, and so, once again, we will simply restate its essence:

> **Fundamentally, risk is an investor's uncertainty about the gains or losses that will result from a particular investment.**

## Principle 4: The Relationship between Governance, Strategy, and Risk

Governance encompasses strategy; strategy encompasses risk. Risk management improves the quality and sustainability of superior returns needed to achieve winning strategies. It includes assuring high-performance work cultures integrating ethical, professional, and industry values and standards, and contributing to a sustainable world. Winning strategies are needed to achieve the performance standards and strategic directions representing the alignment of the firm's stakeholders' interests and efforts, which is the essence of governance.

Validating this principle, consider these data points:
- At a KPMG business roundtable session on governance, it was reported that business leaders want to learn how to integrate *risk* into *strategy*.
- National Association of Corporate Directors (NACD) CEO Ken Daly said, "It's time to weave *strategy* and *risk* into the tapestry of *governance*."
- Dubai Governance Congress Delegates added: Don't forget *social responsibility!*
- And TIAA-CREF state in their Corporate Governance Policy: We believe a top-down commitment to *sound governance principles* reinforces an *ethical business culture* governing all dealings with the firm's *stakeholders*.

Mastering **Principle 4** responds to all of these concerns and the challenges inherent in each.

## Principle 5: The Relationship between Boards, Governance and Shareholders

The board of directors is a governance mechanism available to risk-bearing owners to direct and control the strategic actions of decision-making managers. Other governance mechanisms serving this purpose include executive compensation and multidivisional structures.

Fundamentally, boards are hired by shareholders to direct management's efforts to employ capital by purchasing and operating assets, going through the strategic management process of strategy formulation, organizational design, strategy implementation and modification, *opportunistically* and *episodically*, so that winning strategies are achieved, risk is well-managed, stakeholders' needs and expectations are met, and the firm contributes to a sustainable world.

All this is necessary to deliver long-term shareholder value, which is what boards are responsible for assuring on behalf of the shareholders. By utilizing boards as a mechanism for assuring Strategic Governance throughout the organization, shareholders can now create alignment of stakeholder interests and efforts, providing a systems-based context in which the board can most effectively direct management toward the achievement of this shared goal.

## Principle 6: The Relationship between Boards, Management and Shareholders

All management responsibility is delegated to management by the board on behalf of the shareholders. The so-called "line" between the role of the board and the role of management is determined by the board. The board – not management – has the authority to set the boundaries of its involvement in the business.

This involvement should be whatever is necessary at a given point in time to fulfill the board's fiduciary responsibilities to the shareholders. This is why we now hear of the "floating line" between the role of the board and the role of management. The practice of boards permitting management to set these boundaries is arguably dysfunctional, unprincipled, and unjustifiable.

## Principle 7: The Relationship between Boards, Strategy, and Culture

Strategy and culture are fundamental board responsibilities because of the leverage inherent in these factors. Get them right, and you'll get most other things right. Get them wrong, and it won't matter if you get other things right.

In simple terms, strategy answers the question, "What are we going to do?" and culture answers the question, "How are we going to behave when we do it?" Once these questions are answered and agreed to by the board and management, then and only then has the board created the needed context in which to oversee management in the operations of the business.

## Principle 8: The Relationship between Boards, Management and Strategy

Strategy formulation is a bottom-up and top-down process; an iterative collaboration between the board and management to produce a mutually agreed-upon course of action.

In fulfilling this responsibility, the board must assure actions are taken today that will put the firm in a position of advantage tomorrow. The board's role is to collaborate with management to produce a well-formulated strategy and then assure this strategy is consistently, intensely, and efficiently pursued and, when needed, modified.

According to Sir Adrian Cadbury, former chairman of Cadbury Schweppes plc, this is "far from easy", and requires an "imaginative effort." Strategic Governance is the product of that imaginative effort.

## Principle 9: The Essence of Culture

The essence of culture is adaptability. It must be derived from strategy and then leveraged to enable strategy.

When you manage culture effectively, you make clear what the company expects from your people, and what your people can expect from the company. Who you are as a firm, what you do, and how you do it will be consistently reinforced in all of your management systems, policies and procedures, and daily work. Your organization will be more agile and adaptable than your competitors, responding more effectively and efficiently to problems and opportunities.

There is arguably no better industry than outsourcing to demonstrate the vital need to manage culture as an integral part of organizational design. Firms competing in this global sector must rapidly adapt to the needs and environment of their diverse client base to provide the eco-system effect – all parts working interdependently as a synergistic whole – that companies need to compete in today's global economy. As one speaker said at a 2010 outsourcing event in New York City sponsored by several Philippine organizations including The Business Processing Association (BPA/P), Commission on Information and Communications Technology, BPO Council, Philippine American Chamber of Commerce, and the Consulate General, "Outsourcing relationships begin because of price and service, but they end because of culture and chemistry."

> **When you master the essence of culture, your company will become a high-performance workplace capable of beating the competition quarter after quarter, year after year.**

## Principle 10: The Relationship between Organizational Design and Strategy

Organizational design is part of strategy. What is the point of developing a game plan if you don't have the capability to implement it? In the Strategic Governance System, we always design the ideal organization for the implementation of a given strategy, compare it to the existing organization, and include as part of the strategy, "changing the current organization to look and function like the ideal organization." This is called working *on* the business to enhance the performance of the people working *in* the business, aka *leadership by design*.

# CONCLUSION

In the beginning of this book, we said that Strategic Governance is a reorientation of the individual and global community business experience to account for the existence of an enlightened governance regime, the possibility of achieving it, and the availability of a principle-based system for doing so. We also said we intentionally made this book "short and sweet", so you can master its content. We hope that now, after one or several readings, you will feel motivated enough to "shift into the light", using the Strategic Governance System to achieve extraordinary results on behalf of all of your valued stakeholders

To become a model Strategic Governance firm, we again recommend taking the self-assessment survey, based on the Top Ten Principles of Strategic Governance. This will determine your Strategic Governance Index Score. (SGIS) The score is for tracking purposes only.

We will not be handing out gold stickers or crystal trophies for those with high SGISs. In the future, though, we will enable the investment community to know which firms we feel are practicing the principles of Strategic Governance in ways that will enhance their ability to deliver sustainable, superior returns.

And we do have plans to help create an index fund of model Strategic Governance firms for investors who want to lower risk while earning superior returns. A high SGIS, in and of itself, will not be sufficient to gain admission into this select fund of world-class firms. In addition, we will have to be thoroughly convinced the organization is truly "walking the talk" of Strategic Governance in ways that are sustainable.

# STRATEGIC GOVERNANCE RELATED QUOTES

We add these insightful comments for your further reflection on Strategic Governance:

*Every firm is perfectly designed – for the results it produces.*
**Professor Peter Drucker,**
**The great management guru of the 20th Century**

*Shun the incremental; go for the leap.*
**Jack Welch,**
**GE's legendary CEO**

*What do you see that I'm missing?*
**Livio DeSimone,**
**Former CEO of the innovative leader in manufacturing,**
**3M Company**

*Well-planned change is improving the whole by changing a part.*

**Fred Poses,
Former CEO of American Standard,
an outstanding corporate leader**

*It is more important – and difficult – to install the system in your people's minds than it is to install it in their computers.*

**Eli Goldratt,
Creator of The Theory of Constraints**

*Healthy organizations treat big problems like small ones (and ignore the small problems), while unhealthy organizations treat small problems like big ones (and ignore the big problems).*

**Henry Kissinger,
Former Secretary of State,
a global statecraft strategist**

*All employees have the same job – to assure shareholder value.*

**Fred Poses**

## More about...

*Every firm is perfectly designed –
for the results it produces.*

**Professor Peter Drucker**

This quote – arguably one of Drucker's best – is consistent with Strategic Governance Principle #10: *The Relationship between Organizational Design and Strategy*. Specifically, organizational design is part of strategy precisely because of Drucker's point: We can significantly reduce the risk of failure and increase the probability of success by becoming masters of organizational design, also known as organizational architecture.

This is the essence of leadership by design: Aligning and linking the *skills* and *styles* of the workforce to the management *systems* and organizational *structure* so that the entire organization practices *shared values* derived from *strategy* in ways that enable the firm to implement that *strategy* and create long-term shareholder value. This process is dynamic and ongoing, not static, thereby requiring the systems level of thought and action inherent in the Strategic Governance discipline.

## More about...

*Shun the incremental; go for the leap.*

**Jack Welch**

This Jack Welch quote is consistent with Albert Einstein's observation that, "We can't solve problems by using the same kind of thinking we used to create them." More recently, President Barack Obama expressed the same view by saying, "The old ways that led to this crisis cannot stand" and, "History cannot be allowed to repeat itself."

The problems we are solving with Strategic Governance require business transformation, also known as breakthrough. If your order of change is not big enough, the *status quo* will beat you, causing you to fail as a leader. Strategic Governance is your opportunity to take that leap into a future of extraordinary results that cannot be achieved by incremental improvement along the track you are currently travelling, but instead, can only be achieved by "going for the leap."

## More about...

*What do you see that I'm missing?*

                                                **Livio DeSimone**

As CEO of 3M Company, DeSimone reminded his managers to continuously ask this question and listen carefully to their people's responses. The reason why links right into the previous Welch and Einstein quotes.

We call DeSimone's "everyday, all day" question to the 80,000 employees of 3M "the power question" of Strategic Governance which, in full form, is, *"What's missing for me that, if present, would enable me to achieve a level of performance that right now seems impossible?"* This moves your thinking into the realm of what you don't know that you don't know. ("DKDK") This realm provides infinite possibilities to achieve extraordinary results; results beyond business as usual; results that cannot be predicted by anything done in the past.

Once you reveal what's been missing, you have moved from DKDK to DK. ("Don't Know") You now know what's missing for you – you know what you don't know. The next step in this breakthrough process is to move from DK to "K" ("Know") by learning about this newly found knowledge. Once you know ("K") about that which has been missing, you can now use the tools of the Strategic Governance System to transform this new knowledge into effective actions leading to *extraordinary* results.

Why will the results be extraordinary? Because they come from a place conventional wisdom does not recognize. By managing knowledge this way, ordinary people achieve extraordinary results. This is the breakthrough you are seeking, caused by a new way of thinking (Einstein), revealed by inquiring about what's missing (DeSimone), enabling you to shun the incremental and go for the leap (Welch) in pursuit of an organization perfectly designed to achieve extraordinary results (Drucker). Strategic Governance is *your* means to this end.

## More about...

*Well-planned change is improving the whole by changing a part.*
**Fred Poses**

In 2001, CEO Fred Poses exhorted his 60,000-employee workforce to implement well-planned change at American Standard to make the company better. Poses defined well-planned change as change that "can improve organizations as well as processes" – change to a part of the organization that improves the performance of the whole. In response to Poses' challenge, Larry Costello, senior vice president of human resources, made "Well-Planned Change" the theme of his next HR Leadership meeting.

Costello created an action-based learning session to train and educate American Standard's HR leaders in managing well-planned change, so that they could support the rest of the workforce in developing and implementing well-planned change on a global basis, playing the Strategic Business Partner role. The learning session began with the assertion that well-planned change focuses on the *significant few* processes, not the *trivial many*. The anatomy of the business system was studied to create a shared view of the significant few processes: New product development, order to remittance, cash-to-cash, etc.

**Six Sigma** – a continuous improvement discipline aimed primarily at zero defects – was reviewed as a tool to apply to the significant few work processes. Based on his Allied Signal experience with Six Sigma, Poses launched a Six Sigma movement at American Standard. Creating well-planned change can be achieved when Six Sigma is applied to the right processes at the right time.

The right processes are the significant few processes reflected in the anatomy of the business system. The right time to improve them is when they constrain the productivity of the whole. Processes that are points of constraints on the business system are known as bottlenecks. Six sigma efforts should focus on these bottleneck processes to increase their capacity, thereby increasing the capacity of the entire business system. This approach is consistent with the counter-intuitive wisdom of Stanislaw J. Lec's quote: "The weakest link in a chain is the strongest because it can break it." By strengthening the weakest link, you strengthen the entire chain.

Six Sigma should also be applied to all work processes that produce inputs into bottleneck processes. It is axiomatic that a bottleneck resource should never process a defective input. By increasing the capacity of bottleneck resources, you reduce lead-time for the entire system. By reducing variability and defects of the "up-stream" processes providing essential inputs to the bottlenecks, you increase the error-free output of the entire system. This is how to achieve well-planned change.

Strategic Governance provides you with the systems level of thought and action needed as a prerequisite to practice well-planned change.

## More about...

*It is more important – and difficult – to install the system in your people's minds than it is to install it in their computers.*
**Eli Goldratt**

Goldratt's point is analogous to Drucker's on organizational design. Just as Drucker said your organization must be perfectly designed to produce the targeted result, Goldratt is saying the software system you install in your people's computers must be perfectly designed to be an accelerator of a well-designed management system. If the management system is missing, there is no worthwhile context in which to consider business software. Strategic Governance provides the *management* system needed to effectively leverage the *computer* system.

When Strategic Governance is present, installed in your people's minds, the right technology installed in their computers can be a powerful driver to accelerate positive momentum.

When the Strategic Governance system is missing in your people's minds, technology installed in their computers will most likely accelerate your own self-created demise. *Every organization is perfectly designed – for the results it produces.*

## More about...

*Healthy organizations treat big problems like small ones (and ignore the small problems) while unhealthy organizations treat small problems like big ones (and ignore the big problems).*
**Henry Kissinger**

This issue is directly addressed by Strategic Governance Principle #9: *The Essence of Culture.* The most fundamental purpose of culture is to maximize your supply of adaptability. This enables you and your firm to respond better and faster to the demand for change than the competition.

To maximize your supply of adaptability, you need to manage your firm at the systems level, focusing on alignment, linkage, and interdependence, while eliminating interferences with organizational health and vitality.

When organizations have a limited supply of adaptability, they tend to focus on the so-called "trivial many" problems, what management expert Stephen Covey calls the "gravel in our lives," as opposed to the "significant few" – the "rocks in our lives" – simply because these unhealthy organizations lack the supply of adaptability needed to solve these big problems.

**More about...**

*All employees have the same job –
to assure shareholder value.*

**Fred Poses**

Imagine two companies. One, where the CEO makes this statement (Fred's quote), and everyone understands why it's true and has a shared view of how they work together to perform this shared role successfully on a daily basis. In the second company, the CEO makes this statement, and everyone says, "What's he talking about? We don't have the same jobs. We all work in different functions, different business units, at different organizational levels. We all have different jobs."

All other thing being equal, which company is going to outperform the other?

This is the difference between a *heap* and a *whole*; between an interdependent system focused on enterprise optimization, and an independent hierarchy focused on local optimization. By mastering the Strategic Governance System of purpose, principles, and methodology, your organization will be the high-performing *whole*, reflecting Dr. Deming's aspirations for business organizations: "Everyone working together as a system, with the aim for everybody to win."

## President Barack Obama Quotes

President Barack Obama has demonstrated his ability to clearly state complicated situations in plain English. In 2009, the former law school professors said that "…We ought to set clear rules of the road that promote transparency and accountability…." "That's how we'll make certain that markets reward those who compete honestly and vigorously within the system."

*Transparency, accountability, honesty,* and *vigor* are necessary, but not sufficient. What's missing in President Obama's comments is any reference to **competence.**

He correctly states that, "One of the main reasons this crisis took place is that…no one was responsible for protecting the system as a whole." But are we sure that was the root cause of the problem? Who had the competence to carry out this responsibility successfully if they had been responsible? Anyone come to mind? What exactly is this needed competence? Where has it been applied successfully in the past?

Simply being responsible for something does not require competence; but carrying out a responsibility in an effective manner does. "Protecting the system as a whole" is arguably the primary responsibility of all organizational leaders. Carrying out this responsibility in an effective manner requires the skill of an organizational architect: The ability to lead by design; to create alignment, linkage, and interdependence, so that everyone in the system can win through sustainable means. This is a rare skill, difficult to attain, and therefore frequently *ignored* even though the upside benefit is enormous.

President Obama has told us that what took place in 2008 was a failure of responsibility that allowed Washington to become a place where problems were *ignored* rather than *solved*. But without the missing competence of healthy organizations needed to solve these problems at the root cause level, they will continue to be ignored, as we learned from Secretary Kissinger: *Unhealthy organizations (think: Official Washington) treat small problems like big ones and ignore the big problems.*

To transform unhealthy organizations into healthy ones, ignorance must be replaced with inquiry: *What's missing for me that, if present, would enable me to achieve a level of performance that right now seems impossible?*

Inquiry is the opposite of ignorance. Inquiry is about gaining knowledge; ignorance is about lacking knowledge. Inquiry is about reinvention and renewal; ignorance is about stagnation and demise. Inquiry produces enlightenment, and enlightenment produces responsibility.

For instance, is it possible that, contrary to Obama's assessment, the triumph of ignorance over enlightened inquiry in Washington caused the "failure of responsibility" by preventing a culture of competence and success? If so, the challenge for President Obama is to create an environment of enlightened inquiry in which business leaders willingly *take* responsibility for solving problems and achieving success simply because they've developed the required competence to do so. This is the purpose of Strategic Governance.

In the beginning of this book, we defined Strategic Governance as "a reorientation of the individual and global business community experience to account for the existence of an *enlightened* governance regime...." As you inquire into this enlightened approach to governance, we predict you will feel a new level of freedom and confidence to take responsibility and achieve the extraordinary.

Again in 2009, President Obama said that, "Unfortunately, there are some in the financial industry who are misreading this moment of restored normalcy and that instead of learning the lessons of Lehman [Brothers] and the crisis from which we're still recovering, they're choosing to ignore those lessons...."

Is it possible that the leader of our nation is misreading this a bit himself? If people lack the competence to behave responsibly, what choice do they really have other than to continue doing the best they can? We've seen this happen over and over again.

Let's not confuse intention with capability, even though we can all cite examples of ill-intended leaders, including those at Enron at the beginning of the 21st Century, and more recently, at Goldman Sachs. What's the point in challenging people to do things they are ill-equipped to do? We feel the real lesson to be learned is that business leaders need to become masters of the systems level of thought and action, so they can "protect the system as a whole." The President may want to consider offering Strategic Governance as a tailored-learning solution to our financial, environmental and social sustainability problems, just as President George H.W. Bush offered the Malcolm Baldrige Criteria in the 1980s as a solution to our economic and quality problem.

In this new century and decade, President Obama needs to "lead business leaders through the keyhole of Strategic Governance" so that, when they come out on the other side, they are not only well-intended, but also well-equipped to create a future representing a breakthrough departure from the past that will, as he says, "meet the challenges of this new century."

President Obama is correct in saying that "restoring this responsibility is at the heart of what we must do, even when it's hard to do." This is generally consistent with Sir Adrian Cadbury's assertion that managing strategically, as a system, is hard to do and requires an imaginative effort. Strategic Governance is the product of such an imaginative effort that will enable any business leader willing to become competent in it to "protect the system as a whole" and achieve long-term success.

# APPENDIX

## The Strategic Governance Self-Assessment Survey

The following statements describe the Strategic Governance Principles that enable The Universal Purpose of Corporate Governance.

Please indicate the extent to which these statements reflect your firm's current approach to governance, strategy, risk management, culture and corporate social responsibility.

## Strategic Governance Ratings

### Assign a rating of 1 to 5 per answer as follows:

Strongly Reflects Our Firm's Approach: 1

Solidly Reflects: 2

Somewhat Reflects: 3

Barely Reflects: 4

Does Not At All Reflect: 5

Ratings
(1–5)

_____ 1. The purpose of governance is to align the interests and efforts of stakeholders, establish the firm's strategic direction, assure effective performance of the business, and enable a sustainable eco-system.

_____ 2. The purpose of strategy is to create an integrated and coordinated set of commitments and actions designed to develop strategic assets and then leverage those assets to create sustainable competitive advantages and long-term shareholder value.

_____ 3. Fundamentally, risk is an investor's uncertainty about the gains or losses that will result from a particular investment.

_____ 4. Governance encompasses strategy; strategy encompasses risk.

_____ 5. The board of directors is a governance mechanism available to risk-bearing owners to direct and control the strategic actions of decision-making managers.

_____ 6. All management responsibility is delegated to management by the board on behalf of the shareholders.

_____ 7. Strategy and culture are fundamental board responsibilities.

_____ 8. Strategy formulation is a bottom-up and top-down process; an iterative collaboration between the board and management to produce a mutually agreed-upon strategy.

_____ 9. The purpose of culture is adaptability; it must be derived from strategy and then leveraged to enable strategy.

_____ 10. Organizational design is part of strategy.

## Scoring Outcomes

If you assigned a rating of "1" – award 10 points

If "2" – 8 points

If "3" – 6 points

If "4" – 4 points

If "5" – 2 points

## Total Scoring Categories

For score of 90 – 100 points:
*Model Strategic Governance Organization*

80 – 89:
*Sound Strategic Governance Organization*

70 – 79:
*Directionally Correct Strategic Governance Organization*

50 – 69:
*Immediate Attention Required*

Below 50:
*Urgent Attention Required*

## The Strategic Governance Service

The global economic crisis at the end of the first decade of this new millennium is a failure of past and present governance systems. Box-checking, legislation and regulations may be necessary, but they are definitely not sufficient. In response, we are introducing a breakthrough approach to governance – Strategic Governance – that absolutely fulfills its fundamental purpose: Financial, environmental, and social sustainability.

In a nutshell, Strategic Governance includes a methodology, a system of strategic governance principles, and a universal purpose of corporate governance: Method enabling principles; principles enabling purpose. From this time forward, there is no excuse for repeating the economic fiascos of the past. Financial, environmental, and social sustainability is now a viable choice for every sector, every region, and every firm.

## How Should You Respond?

With bold, decisive action to fully utilize the strategic governance system's unique potential for creating extraordinary results for you, your firm, and its valued stakeholders. This can be done in a two step process:

1. Develop a deep understanding of the meaning and implications of The Universal Purpose of Corporate Governance

2. Develop and implement your own unique, proprietary purpose for corporate governance that aligns with the Universal Purpose while providing your firm with a sustainable competitive advantage.

The primary system for taking these two steps includes the Top Ten Principles of Strategic Governance:

1. The Purpose of Governance
2. The Purpose of Strategy
3. The Essence of Risk
4. The Relationship between Governance, Strategy, and Risk
5. The Relationship between Boards, Governance, and Shareholders
6. The Relationship between Boards, Management, and Shareholders
7. The Relationship between Boards, Strategy, and Culture
8. The Relationship between Boards, Management, and Strategy
9. The Purpose of Culture
10. The Relationship between Organizational Design and Strategy

(These ten principles are discussed in detail beginning on page 77.)

Your mastery and subsequent application of this system of interdependent principles, supported by a related system of models, methods, and techniques, will provide your firm with the holistic capability needed to fulfill the universal governance purpose. This "systems level" of performance will also enable your firm to set and achieve internal standards far greater than any external criteria, thereby complementing the effective role of regulation, legislation, and enforcement: Assuring a principle-based approach to corporate governance.

## Strategic Governance Software: The Silver Lining of Cloud Technology for Business Leaders

*He can take his'n and beat your'n, and then take your'n, and beat his'n.*

**Bum Phillips' assessment of NFL Hall of Fame Coach Don Shula**

Strategic Governance Software is to a business what the central nervous system is to a human being: the ability for the *organization* – not just its people – to think and act intelligently. When you install Strategic Governance into your organization, you will create a business environment where ordinary people can achieve extraordinary results.

For this reason, Strategic Governance Software is the "silver lining of cloud technology" for business leaders, including boards of directors, CEOs, and other members of the "C" suite. Strategic Governance Software will enable these business leaders to view and interact with their organization as a person they are responsible for developing and leading to sustained success:

- What is the competitive environment in which this person will compete?
- What must this person be able to do at a level of excellence to beat the competition and thrive in that environment?
- What capabilities does this person need to have to perform these actions?
- How will these capabilities provide this person with a sustainable competitive advantage?

The purpose of Strategic Governance Software is to equip well-intended business leaders to work *on* their businesses, developing them into intelligent, coordinated, and adaptable organizations, so the people working *in* these businesses consistently beat the competition, exceed the expectations of their stakeholders, and fulfill their responsibility for a sustainable world. Strategic Governance Software will fulfill this purpose by enabling clients to:

- Integrate and coordinate the activities of the board of directors, management, and overall workforce
- Create alignment and linkage between strategy, organization, and operations
- Prioritize work in the context of competitive advantage, long-term shareholder value, and sustainability
- Allocate scarce resources creatively, effectively, and efficiently
- Maximize firm-level performance through positive synergy, where the performance of the whole is greater than the sum performance of the parts
- Manage risk for all the firm's stakeholders.

Summing up the value of Strategic Governance, one of our clients said, while applying it to double the market value of their firm in just two years, "Strategic Governance removes all opportunities to fail."

# ACKNOWLEDGEMENTS

To Professor Mervyn E. King, Chairman of the Board of the Global Reporting Initiative (GRI)

To Jim Kristie, Editor and Associate Publisher, Directors&Boards, a key thought leader in governance

To Debbie Soon, Vice President, Catalyst, a leader in the advancement of women into the corporate boardroom

To Go Sato, Japanese governance expert and former Executive Vice President, Board Director, and Chairman of the Audit Committee – Hitachi Chemical Co., Ltd. in Japan

To Raj Gupta, Board Director – Hewlett-Packard, Tyco International Ltd., The Vanguard Group; Former Chairman, President, and CEO – Rohm and Haas

To Stephen L. Brown, Director & Associate General Counsel of Corporate Governance at TIAA-CREF, an expert and leader in the linkage of corporate governance, social responsibility, and long-term shareholder value

To our colleagues at Drexel University
- Donna DeCarolis
- Walker Tompkins
- Elliott Schreiber

Special thanks to our colleagues in the Middle East, whose conference settings helped to birth this volume: IIR Middle East

To the thought leaders in board leadership, our colleagues at the National Association of Corporate Directors (NACD):
- Ken Daly – National
- Laura Brooks – New Jersey
- Marty Coyne – New Jersey
- Bill McCracken – National and New Jersey
- Jim Fraser – North Carolina (Research Triangle)
- Chris Mitchell – Southern California
- Ed and Chuck Merino – Southern California
- Ron Poelman – Utah
- Kelly Dodd – Texas TriCities

To the thought leaders in corporate and issuer financial management and reporting at Financial Executives International (FEI):
- Marie N. Hollein
- Paul W. Chase
- Cheryl Graziano
- Liliana Devita
- Jim Eagan
- Gregory Dolecki

To Curt Crawford, Director, E. I. du Pont de Nemours, ITT, ON Semiconductor, and Agilysys

To our colleagues in the DuPont organization, a market-driven science company:
- Lisa Johnson
- Usha Gopalratnam

## ACKNOWLEDGEMENTS

To my brother Michael Sickles

To my wife and business partner and lifelong helpmate Mary Ann Boerner

To our colleagues at the Governance & Accountability Institute – who are so helpful in shepherding this volume toward completion:
- Amy Gallagher
- Lou Coppola
- Peter Hamilton
- Ken Cynar

And to all of the thought leaders who are un-named but who have contributed mightily to this effort – thank you for your efforts in inspiring us by sharing your knowledge and experience.

# About Governance & Accountability Institute

The Institute is a service organization that manages knowledge focused on ESG (the environmental, social and governance key performance indicators of corporations) and Sustainability issues. The Institute provides timely news, actionable research and information, a range of perspectives and opinion, reliable data, and customized advisory services to organizations, institutions and individuals seeking to do the right thing for the right reasons.

**On the Web: www.GA-Institute.com**

## About Accountability-Central.com

This public access news, opinion and research platform is published by the Institute, delivering important content through specific accountability content silos on the topics of ESG and Sustainability, corporate governance, social investing, shareholder activism, financial reporting, ethics, and others.

**On the Web: www.Accountability-Central.com**

## About SustainabilityHQ™

The Institute's premium subscription-based knowledge management platform focuses on ESG and Sustainability issues of importance to investors (asset owners and managers), financial analysts / researchers in the investment community, and corporate management and boards of directors. Topic categories include ESG / Sustainability, Sovereign Wealth Funds, USA Public Sector Employee Retirement Funds and Systems, and ESG Asset Managers.

**On the Web: www.SustainabilityHQ.com**

## About the Authors

Hank Boerner and Mark W. Sickles are Fellows of Governance & Accountability Institute.

**Hank Boerner** is Chairman and CEO of Governance & Accountability Institute, a New York-based global research, news monitoring, knowledge management and strategic advisory services provider organization, serving clients in the corporate sector, capital markets, public sector and not-for-profit sector.

He has been a business strategist and management consultant and advisor for more than 25 years, frequently assisting clients with issues in management services and programs, and response to critical events and crises situations. His areas of expertise include: public and institutional governance, shareholder activism, sustainable and responsible investment, disclosure and transparency, corporate social responsibility, third-party engagement, and capital markets activities. The Institute monitors global trends in ESG and Sustainability investing, and corporate responsibility. Contact Hank at **hboerner@ga-institute.com**.

**Mark W. Sickles** is an organizational architect, advisor to corporate directors and executives, author, and keynote speaker. Known as the creator of the globally renowned Shareholder Value Assurance (SVA) methodology, Mark has provided the global business community with a superior governance regime by integrating governance, strategy, risk, culture and social responsibility. He is rapidly becoming one of the most influential people in the world on this critical topic of strategic governance.

Over the years, Mark has practiced SVA and Strategic Governance to create billions of dollars of shareholder value as a senior executive, officer, director, and external consultant. As one client said, "Mark took away our opportunities to fail," leading to a dramatic increase in profitability and doubling the firm's market value in just two years. Contact Mark at **msickles@ga-institute.com**.

## Book Cover Explanation

Our cover and this page illustrate two natural examples of the breakthrough opportunity that Strategic Governance provides: Swarming Intelligence (SI). Bird flocking and fish schooling are examples of SI organizations in which the performance of the whole is not merely greater but, more notably, different than the sum performance of its parts.

SI organizations have been called mysterious – even magical. Without any apparent control structure, the intelligence of the whole supervenes on its parts, causing individual performance one would never predict or anticipate that, in turn, causes the whole organization to consistently succeed in dynamic, competitive, even harsh environments.

While this principle-based system of organizational intelligence is naturally present in flocks of birds and schools of fish, it is naturally missing in human organizations like yours. Strategic Governance is your opportunity to change that.

Photo credits:
school of fish: ©Andy Chia, Dreamstime.com
swirling fish: ©Melvinlee, Dreamstime.com
flock of starlings: ©Digoarpi, Dreamstime.com